Su-27 Flanker™

Official Secrets & Solutions

Now Available

Computer Game Books

1942: The Pacific Air War—The Official Strategy Guide

The 11th Hour: The Official Strategy Guide

The 7th Guest: The Official Strategy Guide

Aces Over Europe: The Official Strategy Guide

Across the Rhine: The Official Strategy Guide

Alone in the Dark 3: The Official Strategy Guide

Armored Fist: The Official Strategy Guide

Ascendancy: The Official Strategy Guide

Blackthorne: The Official Strategy Guide

CD-ROM Games Secrets, Volume 1

Celtic Tales: Balor of the Evil Eye—The Official Strategy Guide

Cyberia: The Official Strategy Guide

Computer Adventure Games Secrets

Descent: The Official Strategy Guide

DOOM Battlebook

DOOM II: The Official Strategy Guide

Dracula Unleashed: The Official Strategy Guide & Novel

Dragon Lore: The Official Strategy Guide

Dungeon Master II: The Legend of Skullkeep—The Official Strategy Guide

Fleet Defender: The Official Strategy Guide

Frankenstein: Through the Eyes of the Monster—The Official Strategy Guide

Front Page Sports Football Pro '95: The Official Playbook

Hell: A Cyberpunk Thriller—The Official Strategy Guide

Heretic: The Official Strategy Guide

I Have No Mouth and I Must Scream: The Official Strategy Guide

In The 1st Degree: The Official Strategy Guide

The Journeyman Project 2: Buried in Time—The Official Strategy Guide

Kingdom: The Far Reaches—The Official Strategy Guide

King's Quest VII: The Unauthorized Strategy Guide

The Legend of Kyrandia: The Official Strategy Guide

Lords of Midnight: The Official Strategy Guide

Machiavelli the Prince: Official Secrets & Solutions

Marathon: The Official Strategy Guide

Master of Orion: The Official Strategy Guide

Master of Magic: The Official Strategy Guide

Mech Warrior 2: The Official Strategy Guide

Microsoft Arcade: The Official Strategy Guide

Microsoft Flight Simulator 5.1: The Official Strategy Guide

Microsoft Golf: The Official Strategy Guide

Microsoft Space Simulator: The Official Strategy Guide

Might and Magic Compendium: The Authorized Strategy Guide for Games I, II, III, and IV

Myst: The Official Strategy Guide, Revised Edition

Online Games: In-Depth Strategies and Secrets

Oregon Trail II: The Official Strategy Guide

Outpost: The Official Strategy Guide

The Pagemaster: Official CD-ROM Strategy Guide

Panzer General: The Official Strategy Guide

Perfect General II: The Official Strategy Guide

Power Pete: Official Secrets and Solutions

Prince of Persia: The Official Strategy Guide

Prisoner of Ice: The Official Strategy Guide

Rebel Assault: The Official Insider's Guide

Return to Zork Adventurer's Guide

Romance of the Three Kingdoms IV: Wall of Fire—The Official Strategy Guide

Shadow of the Comet: The Official Strategy Guide

Sid Meier's Civilization, or Rome on 640K a Day

Sid Meier's Colonization: The Official Strategy Guide

SimCity 2000: Power, Politics, and Planning

SimEarth: The Official Strategy Guide

SimFarm Almanac: The Official Guide to SimFarm

SimLife: The Official Strategy Guide

SimTower: The Official Strategy Guide

SubWar 2050: The Official Strategy Guide

Terry Pratchett's Discworld: The Official Strategy Guide

Thunderscape: The Official Strategy Guide

TIE Fighter: The Official Strategy Guide

TIE Fighter: Defender of the Empire—Official Secrets & Solutions

Ultima: The Avatar Adventures

Ultima VII and Underworld: More Avatar Adventures

Under a Killing Moon: The Official Strategy Guide

WarCraft: Orcs & Humans Official Secrets & Solutions

Warlords II Deluxe: The Official Strategy Guide

Wing Commander I, II, and III: The Ultimate Strategy Guide

X-COM Terror From The Deep: The Official Strategy Guide

X-COM UFO Defense: The Official Strategy Guide

X-Wing: Collector's CD-ROM—The Official Strategy Guide

How to Order:

For information on quantity discounts contact the publisher: Prima Publishing, P.O. Box 1260BK, Rocklin, CA 95677-1260; (916) 632-4400. On your letterhead include information concerning the intended use of the books and the number of books you wish to purchase. For individual orders, turn to the back of the book for more information.

Su-27 Flanker™

Official Secrets & Solutions

Tom Basham

PRIMA PUBLISHING

Project Editor: Chris Balmain

ISBN: 0-7615-0546-6
Library of Congress Catalog Card Number: 95-73071
Printed in the United States of America
96 97 98 99 DD 10 9 8 7 6 5 4 3 2 1

For my wife, Sara

Contents

Chapter 5   Mission Planning and Campaign Strategies . . 73

Appendix A   Air-to-Air Weapons Comparison 99

Appendix B   Metric Conversion 105

Index 107

CHAPTER ONE

Orientation
Checkride

The demise of the Cold War opened doors into Warsaw Pact countries that had been sealed for decades. Many new, previously unthinkable opportunities appeared overnight, including the use of MiG-29s as front-line NATO aircraft and the appearance of a highly detailed, extremely realistic Su-27 flight simulation!

To some degree, "flying is flying." That is, if you've learned to successfully fight a Western-built fighter such as an F-16, you've already learned many of the basics needed to successfully pilot an Su-27. There are, however, many things the Western simulations haven't prepared you for, especially considering that *Su-27* exclusively uses an authentic, completely Cyrillic, Russian cockpit design.

This book does not teach you the secret trick to winning each mission. Instead, this book endeavors to explain *how to fly an Su-27 in combat.* There is, however, no substitute for practice. If you want to be an ace combat jock, you must practice, practice, practice, and then practice some more. It won't matter how closely you read this book—if you don't practice the techniques until you see them in your sleep you will not master the Su-27.

You will see numerous references to the MiG-29 throughout this book. Although the Suhkoi and MiG designers bristle at suggestions they copied each other's designs, one cannot ignore the many similarities between the two aircraft and the Soviet doctrine under which both aircraft served.

The Su-27's Combat Role

First and foremost, you must understand the strengths and limitations of the Su-27. If you remember only one thing from this book remember this: The Su-27 is not an F-16. It does not fly like an F-16, it does not handle like an F-16, and if you try to fly it like an F-16 you will get shot out of the simulated sky every time.

For decades, Soviet pilots relied heavily on GCI, or *Ground Controlled Intercept*, controllers to guide them to their targets. Onboard radars were unable to search out, detect, and track enemy targets. Further, in Central Europe, the Soviets maintained a "quantity over quality"

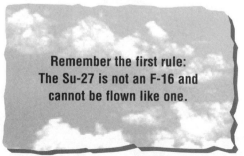

Remember the first rule: The Su-27 is not an F-16 and cannot be flown like one.

approach. While NATO planners expected F-15s and F-16s to dogfight their way through 1-against-10 odds and win, the Soviets took an arguably more realistic view: They'd launch hordes of fighters in waves at the front lines, fire a massive volley of missiles in the enemy's face, then turn and run while the next wave advanced. For the most part, ground radar (GCI) sites guided the Soviet aircraft to their targets. Soviet tactical doctrine stressed conformity over initiative. "Just do as you are told, Comrade."

Changing of the Guard?

The Soviets realized all along, however, that their technology must move forward regardless of the size of their inventory. Could 100 MiG-21s defeat 20 F-22s in the war of the future? Probably not, but 100 MiG-29s arguably could hold their own with 5-to-1 numerical superiority. New aircraft would be needed. Further, the Soviets were painfully aware of the threat air-launched anti-radiation missiles, or ARMs, posed to their fixed, GCI sites. Walls of fighters in the sky were useless if they couldn't find their targets because the GCI site was destroyed.

Then, in the Soviet Union's waning years, several new, advanced aircraft entered the scene: MiG-29, Su-27, and MiG-31. Generally speaking, the MiG-29 is regarded as a superb dogfighter, the Su-27 as an outstanding dog-fighter, and the MiG-31 as a "mini AWACS." At first glance, it would appear the Soviets had revised their doctrine and looked to match technology with technology. This perception is furthered by a few ex-Soviet pilots who, thanks to the demise of the Cold War, have the opportunity to make themselves heard in the West, leading many to conclude the current generation of Soviet-built aircraft are superfighters.

A Realistic Appraisal

Myths often grow from a kernel of truth, and the Su-27 myth is no exception. The Su-27 is an outstanding aircraft in some regards, but has serious short-comings. SSI's Su-27 simulation does an outstanding job of portraying the real aircraft; if you know how to exploit its strengths and avoid its weaknesses you'll find the Su-27 a marvelous weapons platform. If, however, you try to fly the aircraft according to its purported abilities, you'll be sorely disappointed with its performance. It is extremely important, therefore, to understand the Su-27s strengths, limitations, and weaknesses.

GCI or Initiative?

The comments of a few former Soviet pilots indicate that heavy reliance on ground controllers is itself a myth. The reunification of Germany, however, sheds a different light on the situation. Forty-two former East German MiG-29 pilots applied to remain in the unified *Luftwaffe*. Right away, Western instructors noticed the MiG-29 pilots were not using the aircraft to fullest potential. The MiG-29 pilots initially resented the Western know-it-all attitude until Western instructors began dogfighting aging F-4 Phantoms against the MiG-29s . . . and won.

The MiG-29 pilots were used to GCI coordinators choreographing every move, telling them where to fly, even how to set cockpit switches. They flew standardized maneuvers and relied on instructions from the ground instead of relying on initiative. Trained under the Soviet machine, these pilots were guided to a point in the air by ground controllers, launched their weapons, and turned for home. The overwhelming body of evidence disputes any claims of initiative or tactical freedom within the Soviet system.

Of the 42 East German pilots, only 13 survived the transition from Eastern to Western tactics. They weren't trained to maximize their aircraft performance, nor were they taught to lead a group of aircraft, direct them through the battle, and bring them all home. Although they initially epitomized the rigidity of the Soviet system, those who survived the training became formidable dogfighters and vocal proponents of the Western system.

Rely on initiative to defeat the enemy.

Superfighter or Dud?

A commonly asked question in today's post-Cold War world is: *If the Soviets merely intended to launch clouds of missiles from walls of fighters, why then did they build such capable dogfighters?* The current generation aircraft are superfighters in some respects, but fall short in others. Don't simply label the Su-27 "superfighter" or "dud," but realize that it excels in some aspects and falters in others.

Helmet-Mounted Sights

First, let's examine the helmet-mounted sight system (HMS). Western pilots who have had the opportunity to fly mock engagements against HMS-equipped aircraft report in *Air Forces Monthly* magazine, "We have found (the HMS system) is not as lethal as we expected." Although presenting a formidable threat which must be respected, it is not an insurmountable one.

The HMS, coupled with off-boresight missile capability, gives the Su-27 a wider launch envelope than most Western fighters, but it has its limitations. It is particularly effective taking a shot across the circle in a turning fight, but *it's not a silver bullet.* It can't save you if you've let the enemy camp on your 6 o'clock position. You can use this capability to "cut the corner" when you're on the offense or neutral, letting you take a shot your opponent probably can't take, but the capability is no substitute for dogfighting skills.

> The HMS and off-boresight missile capability are formidable threats, but they are not silver bullets. You must learn to use this capability in conjunction with your dogfighting skills instead of relying on it to save you from all bandits.

Avionics

MiG-29 and Su-27 avionics generally are regarded as inadequate. Primarily, the Su-27 (and the MiG-29, for that matter) can lock only one target at a time. Additionally, the Su-27 can only track a limited number of targets at one time (10). Worse, the Su-27's radar cannot scan for additional aircraft while locked onto a target. Last, the cockpit uses a complex layout, making radar operation and target locking a difficult task.

There are, however, some very bright spots to consider. The radar has a reported detection range of 240km (149 miles) and tracking range of 185 km (115 miles). The Su-27 remains datalinked with GCI and AWACS aircraft which keep track of the "big picture" for the Su-27 pilot. Further, the radar is backed by an electro-optical system combining a laser range finder and IRST (Infrared Search and Track) system with a reported range of 50 km (31 miles).

As a simulated Su-27 pilot you have two avionics-related concerns: First, you rely heavily on GCI and AWACS datalinks to keep you informed. If these items are present you receive a 360-degree, "God's-eye" view of the battlefield, including objects located behind you. If, however, you lose these datalinks, you lose that view. Without datalinks, your view of the world contracts significantly. This is primarily a concern during the first phase of combat, when you're trying to locate a specific target and maneuver into optimal attack position. In a tight dogfight, you won't be looking down at the radar display anyway.

> **Always ensure GCI or AWACS support is available. Always protect GCI and AWACS sites from enemy attacks.**

Second, Su-27 cockpit ergonomics leave something to be desired. In fact, it is quite difficult to operate the radar, requiring the pilot to remove his hands from the flight controls and operate switches around the cockpit. It is difficult and time-consuming to lock targets. You will see this during combat. It is important that you fully understand the limitations of the avionics suite so you can properly maneuver the aircraft.

> **Learn the limitations of the avionics suite and the demands those limitations place on aircraft maneuvering.**

Flight Performance

The Su-27 can hold its own in this category, but again, it is not a "wonder plane" capable of working miracles. The Su-27 snatched several time-to-altitude records from the F-15, but recall that the Su-27 in question was chained to the runway, the engines spooled up to full afterburner, then sprung loose down the runway, significantly cutting its takeoff roll (and thereby reducing its time to altitude).

Your biggest advantage is thrust. You've got a lot of power in those two turbofan engines. The aircraft maneuvers well and an expert pilot can hold his own in a knife fight, but make no mistake about it: This is no F-16. You can't roll the wings 90 degrees, yank the stick in your lap, and hope to out-turn every adversary.

Thrust has a price—fuel. Running at full afterburner gives you a lot of thrust, but guzzles fuel at an alarming rate. It'll bleed speed under high G and

> While the Su-27 has sufficient thrust to hold its own in a dogfight, it doesn't have the flight performance of an F-16. You must fight "smarter" instead of "harder."

depart into a nasty, altitude-consuming spin if you're not careful. You can yank 9 G in this aircraft, but you must learn when to use that capability and when to use other tactics. In general, try to fly smarter (using less G-loads) than harder (using higher G-loads).

Conclusion

The Su-27 is an incredible aircraft with amazing capabilities (we explore these in greater detail later). You must understand, however, that this is not a dogfight game and the Su-27 is not intended as a close-range knife-fighter. Dispel any notions of diving into a cluster of F-16s and turning and burning them into the ground or you'll find yourself riding the "silk elevator" back home every time. Instead, this book examines how to exploit the Flanker's strengths while avoiding its weaknesses. Don't expect a few technical innovations, such as the HMS, to solve all your combat problems. Instead, this book explains how and when to use those systems to your advantage.

CHAPTER TWO

Basic
Flight
Training

Know Thy Airplane

To successfully employ any weapons platform you must understand fully the handling characteristics of that platform. The Su-27 is no exception. This chapter supplements the *Su-27 Flanker* manual. Where the manual explains takeoff, landing, and spin-recovery parameters, this chapter actually walks you through each of these procedures, explaining exactly how to initiate, execute, or recover from the specified procedure.

Takeoff Procedures

Takeoff procedures vary somewhat based on payload, weather, and equipment failure (such as engine failure).

Normal Takeoff Checklist

Make sure you properly configure your aircraft prior to takeoff. Remember, also, that to conserve fuel Russian pilots don't normally engage afterburner on takeoff.

Normal Takeoff Procedures Checklist

❏ 1. *Taxi into position and hold.* Taxi to the end of the launching runway, turn onto the runway and line up with the center line, then stop.

❏ 2. *Increase MFD range.* Set the MFD range to its maximum display range. Do not activate the radar or EOS yet.

❏ 3. *Lower the Flaps.* Increase all specified takeoff speeds by 30 km/hr if flaps are unavailable or unused.

❏ 4. *Engage the wheelbrake.* Note that you must hold the Ⓦ key down.

❏ 5. *Verify control surfaces.* Switching to the outside view, verify that the appropriate control surfaces move when you move the stick and rudders.

❏ 6. *Apply full military power.* Increase throttles to 100 percent. Do not engage afterburner.

❏ 7. *Release the wheelbrake.*

❏ 8. *(Optional) Engage afterburners for maximum performance takeoff.* Not recommended for normal operational procedures.

❏ 9. *Rotate at 250 km/hr.* For takeoffs with a launch weight under 28,000 kg, at 250 km/hr pull back gently on the stick until the nose wheel lifts off (this is called "rotating"). Main gear should lift off around 280 to 300 km/hr. For takeoff weights over 28,000 kg, rotate at 300 km/hr with main gear lift off between 320 and 350 km/hr.

❏ 10. *Gear up at positive ROC.* Raise gear when the altimeter indicates a positive Rate of Climb (ROC).

❏ 11. *Execute climb out to altitude.*

Single-Engine Takeoff Checklist

Single-engine takeoffs are extremely dangerous. You have several options available to you depending on the launch weight of your aircraft, when the engine failure occurs, and the size of obstacles beyond the opposite end of the runway. Table 2-1 indicates emergency options based on aircraft launch weight:

Table 2-1: Single-Engine Takeoff Success Probabilities Based on Aircraft Weight	
Launch Weight	**Success Probability**
Under 23,000 kg	Marginal
23,000 kg to 25,000 kg	Unlikely
25,000 kg to 28,000 kg	Very Unlikely
Over 28,000 kg	Extremely Unlikely

As you can see from the table, single-engine takeoffs are difficult even at relatively light weights. Under 23,000 kg the aircraft will become airborne; the problem is *keeping* it airborne. When operating on only one engine, the Su-27 will descend during straight-and-level flight. That is, if you keep the nose right on the horizon, the aircraft will descend. Further, every time you pitch the nose up or execute a turn, you bleed speed. The trick, therefore, is controlling how much speed you bleed. If you can maintain 300 km/hr, you can probably bring the aircraft back for a landing. If you drop below 250 km/hr, you're probably going for a swim. In general, try to keep a gentle climb going, grab as much altitude as you can, then turn back and attempt a landing.

WARNING:
Do not attempt a single-engine takeoff if launch weight exceeds 28,000 kg!

Failure Prior to Takeoff Roll

Your options also vary depending on *when* the failure occurs. If the failure occurs before you begin the takeoff roll (before step 7 of the "Normal Takeoff Procedures Checklist") you have the widest number of available options. First, you can choose to simply abort the mission. This is, obviously, the safest and usually wisest course of action. Second, you can assess the current situation and determine the odds completing the mission on a single engine. Under these circumstances you must assess two factors:

1. *Launch Weight.* What is the launch weight of your aircraft? Can you safely execute a single-engine takeoff? As explained in table 2-1, your success chances diminish as launch weight increases over 23,000 kg.

2. *Mission Requirements.* Can you complete the mission on a single engine? Forget any thoughts of dogfighting with only one engine; you simply do not have sufficient thrust. If you carry long-ranged air-to-air missiles you might successfully intercept a slow-moving target (such as a tanker or AWACS) but you'll lack the acceleration to escape the combat zone at any reasonable speed. If enemy fighters appear on the scene, you'll be a sitting duck. Reduced speed also makes you an easier target for surface-to-air defenses, putting you at higher risk during ground attack missions.

If you can execute a takeoff and still complete the mission, then you might consider performing the mission with only one engine.

Remember, the afterburner will not engage when you have only one active engine in an effort to reduce asymmetrical yaw. This further reduces available thrust.

Single-Engine Takeoff Checklist

☐ 1. *Taxi into position and hold.* Taxi to the end of the launching runway, turn onto the runway and line up with the center line, then stop.

☐ 2. *Increase MFD range.* Set the MFD range to its maximum display range. Do not activate the radar or EOS yet.

☐ 3. *Lower the Flaps.* Increase all specified takeoff speeds by 30 km/hr if flaps are unavailable or unused.

☐ 4. *Engage the wheelbrake.* Note that you must hold down the ⓦ key.

☐ 5. *Verify control surfaces.* Switching to the outside view, verify that the appropriate control surfaces move when you move the stick and rudders.

☐ 6. *Apply full military power.* Increase throttles to 100 percent. Note that afterburners will not engage with a single operational engine.

☐ 7. *Release the wheelbrake.*

☐ 8. *Rotate at 280 km/hr.* For takeoffs with a launch weight under 28,000 kg, keep the nose wheel on the runway until you reach 280 km/hr, then pull back gently on the stick until the nose wheel lifts off. Main gear should lift off by 300 km/hr. If the main gear has not lifted off by 320 km/hr, immediately abort the takeoff (see takeoff abort checklist).

Single-engine takeoffs are not recommended for aircraft weighing over 28,000 kg. Aircraft weighing over 28,000 kg should rotate at 300 km/hr and lift off by 350 km/hr.

☐ 9. *Apply Rudder.* Apply rudder toward the *good engine* to offset asymmetrical yaw. Watch the turn-and-slip indicator. Apply rudder *toward* the ball until it is centered in the indicator.

☐ 10. *Gear up at positive ROC.* Raise gear when the altimeter indicates a positive *Rate of Climb* (ROC).

☐ 11. *Immediately jettison stores as necessary to maintain flight.*

☐ 12. *Maintain a wings-level climb to 1,500 m.* Keep the aircraft's nose pointed above the horizon (do not stall the aircraft!). Do not bank the aircraft; banking reduces the amount of lift being used in the climb. Maximize climb rate, without stalling, in preparation for a single-engine landing. Climb to 1500 meters before beginning any turns.

Because the afterburner won't light on the good engine, losing a single engine decreases total thrust output by more than just 50 percent. It becomes quite difficult to recover speed lost in turns. Do not attempt any steep turns at below 500 m with only one working engine. You will lose both speed and altitude, neither of which you can recover.

Failure During Takeoff Roll

If you've already begun the takeoff roll when one engine goes down, you must immediately assess acceleration versus your current speed. Obviously, the best choice is to abort the takeoff roll.

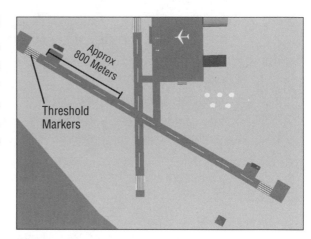

Figure 2-1 Runway Length Approximation

Takeoff Abort Checklist

☐ 1. *Immediately ascertain remaining runway length.* Under normal circumstances the Su-27 requires a 620 m landing roll. If less than 600 m of runway remains and your speed is between 200 and 270 km/hr, *eject immediately.* As shown in figure 2-1, you can estimate runway length by the centerline hash marks. Three hash marks equal roughly 600 m.
   If your speed exceeds 270 km/hr, consider proceeding with the takeoff instead of aborting.

☐ 2. *Immediately reduce power.* Reduce throttles to minimum.

☐ 3. *Engage wheelbrake.* Remember to *hold* the wheelbrake key.

☐ 4. *Deploy drag chute.* Release the drag parachute as quickly as possible.

☐ 5. *Deploy airbrakes and flaps.* Increase drag as much as possible to help slow the aircraft.

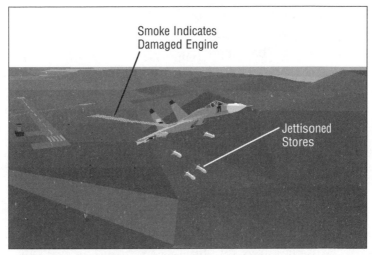

Figure 2-2 The trail of smoke indicates an engine failure just after takeoff. The pilot already is jettisoning stores to lighten the aircraft.

Failure After Takeoff

If you lose an engine just after takeoff (or execute a single-engine takeoff), typically you should return to base and land immediately. If you cannot maintain a climb sufficient to clear any obstacles, immediately jettison stores.

Takeoff Procedures Conclusion

When your equipment works properly, takeoffs are quite easy. When something goes wrong, however, they can become quite deadly. Engine failure during takeoffs and landings have cost many pilots their lives, mainly because the aircraft is so low at the time of the failure. Under such circumstances, altitude equals time. The more altitude you have, the more time you have to decide what to do. At low altitude, you must immediately make a series of correct decisions: One bad decision and it's all over but the funeral.

Landing Procedures

Landings are generally quite a bit more difficult than takeoffs. Even when everything works, landings require far more precision and control. When things don't work right, landings become quite difficult. What can go wrong during landing? Several things: an engine fails suddenly during approach; you encounter a severe crosswind; battle-damaged systems won't respond properly; or the pilot sets up a bad approach.

As the manual explained, the secret to all good landings is the approach. If you cut corners on the approach, the landing will suffer. Unless you're low on fuel or sustained significant battle damage, always take the time to select the **BO3B** HUD mode, fly to the initial approach point, and follow the ILS in.

Reverse the Controls

Normally, you use throttle to control speed while using the stick to control the aircraft's attitude. If you want to climb, you pull back on the stick. If you want to slow down, you reduce power. During landings, however, the procedure reverses. During landings, use the stick to control airspeed and the throttle to control altitude. How? It's simple, really. To slow down, pitch the aircraft up. To speed up, lower the nose. To climb, increase power; to descend, decrease power. Figure 2-3 shows that it can be done.

Practice the control technique before trying an actual landing. Take an Su-27 up to 5,000 meters, level off and reduce speed. Keep the aircraft's nose on the horizon as speed decreases. Watch the angle-of-attack indicator. As speed decreases, AOA increases; eventually the aircraft begins descending. Now, take your hand completely off the throttle. Maintain a constant speed, say 300 km/hr, as you descend. If you accelerate too much, pull back on the stick to slow the aircraft. If you slow too much, push the nose over to accelerate. It takes some practice; new pilots often pull back too hard and stall the aircraft. If the aircraft climbs when you pull back on the stick, you're going too fast. Work the stick very gently as the aircraft descends, maintaining a constant speed as altitude drops.

Once you've mastered that, climb back to 5,000 m and try the opposite. Point the nose up about 25 degrees (causing you to climb). Reduce throttle until the climb rate decreases. Keeping the nose pitched up 25 degrees, cut the throttle back further until the aircraft stops climbing. Still keeping the nose up, reduce throttle even further until the aircraft begins to descend. Pick an altitude (say 5,000 meters) and hold the aircraft there while keeping the nose pitched up. If you climb above 5,000, cut the throttle and descend. If you descend below 5,000, increase power. Repeat the exercise until you can hold a constant altitude with the aircraft's nose pitched up.

Patience is the key. Remember to make small adjustments, then give

Positive
Pitch
Angle

Negative
Vertical
Velocity

Figure 2-3 It can be done: Despite the positive bank angle, the HUD shows this Su-27 descending.

them time to take effect. Don't respond too quickly to the instruments; they take time to update. If you "chase the instruments" you'll find yourself making bigger and bigger corrections. Eventually, overcorrecting ruins the approach and forces you to go around for another try.

Crosswind Landing Procedures

A wind blowing across the width of the runway is called a *crosswind*. Crosswinds work to push the aircraft left or right as it lines up with the runway.

Typically, most airfields situate several runways at odd angles such that the wind cannot cross them both simultaneously. In severe wind conditions you may need to divert to an airfield with correctly situated runways.

Figure 2-4 shows the typical result of a crosswind on landing.

> **Always check the Met Report in the Options menu and record any reported winds before taking off. You have no way to determine wind status while airborne.**

Figure 2-4 A strong crosswind pushes this Su-27 away from the runway.

The pilot did not compensate sufficiently and the wind blew the aircraft past the runway while the pilot tried to align it.

Slipping and Skidding

Many simulator pilots tend to move the nose around with the rudders during landing. If the aircraft isn't quite lined up, they press the rudders until the nose points right at the runway. This, of course, points the aircraft but doesn't change its heading immediately. Momentum carries it along its original heading until the engine's thrust establishes a new heading. During this time, the aircraft is *slipping* (also called *crabbing*).

    The same computer pilots typically respond to crosswinds by flying toward the runway against the wind, then stomping the rudder and crabbing their aircraft to the runway just before touchdown. In the real world such tactics can damage the aircraft or even result in a crash, depending on how much the pilot crabs the aircraft. *Su-27* accurately and realistically models landing procedures, including crosswind landings, and won't tolerate extremely poor landings. If you don't touch down properly, you'll crash. As the manual explains, flying into the wind throughout the approach works better than the "crab" method described above.

Complications

It's fairly easy to master crosswind landings by themselves, assuming the crosswind isn't hurricane-strength. They do, however, offer other complications. A crosswind in conjunction with an engine failure (or other battle damage) can turn a difficult situation into an impossible one. It's extremely important that you check the Met Report in the Options menu prior to flight and record the wind status. Two kilometers out on final approach with an engine down is no place to suddenly learn of a crosswind you didn't correct for!

Engine-Out Landings

Single-engine landings are inherently dangerous. You're low to the ground and you can't climb away if things go wrong. You've got one chance to set up the approach correctly, and you must *maintain* the approach all the way in. A single mistake at any juncture is quite often fatal.

As with all landings, success lies in the approach. If you begin an engine-out landing from a bad position you stand little chance of salvaging it later. Ideally, you need to intercept the initial approach point, located by using the **BO3B** or "Return" HUD mode, at 1,000 m altitude and around 450 km/hr airspeed. If you lose the engine midway through the mission, you must grab as much altitude as you can on egress. If you're too high when you reach the initial approach point you can always dive it away.

As the manual explains, the correct path you normally follow down to the runway is called the *glideslope*. You can't climb away at will, so falling beneath the glideslope puts you in a bad situation. It is advisable, therefore, that you fly single-engine landings above the glideslope all the way in. It's easy enough to scrub off altitude toward the end, and you can always land a *little long*— that is, farther down the runway than normal. You may not have enough runway to stop completely, but running off the pavement and getting stuck in the grass is better than crashing.

The problem, therefore, amounts to controlling your *sink rate*. You can't sink too fast during the descent or you'll crash short of the runway. If you don't sink fast enough, you'll float right past the runway and crash beyond it. Of course, even if you land on the runway, if you're sinking too fast the main

Figure 2-5 Note how long this damaged Su-27 landed.

gear will collapse and you'll still crash. Generally, vertical velocity should be less than -2 m/s at touchdown. If you sink much faster than that you'll crash.

I recommend you maintain your altitude about 20 percent above the specified glideslope. Divide the specified altitude on the HUD by 10, then multiply by 2, then add that to the altitude on the HUD. For example, if the glideslope display on the HUD calls for 500 meters, divide that by 10 (getting 50), multiply by 2 (resulting in 100), and add that to 500 (producing 600). Try to maintain 600 meters, therefore, instead of 500 at that particular point. If the HUD calls for 100 meters, maintain 120 meters, at 60 maintain 72, and so on. This gives you a margin of error above the glideslope causing you to land long. Landing long, though, is preferable to landing in the weeds.

Landings Conclusion

Good landings are the mark of a truly professional pilot. Almost anyone can learn to put an airplane on the pavement on a clear, sunny day. It takes more skill to land on the runway centerline every time, and it takes considerable experience to bring a wounded aircraft back in a high crosswind. Regardless of the dogfighting kills you score and the ground targets you destroy, only when you can land your aircraft every time are you truly a "simulation pilot."

The Edge of the Envelope

Chapter 3 of the manual details basic aerodynamic principles and briefly describes stalls and spins. To elaborate, the angle between the aircraft's heading and the airflow is called *angle of attack* (AOA). Anytime the aircraft changes heading, it rotates about its center of gravity and points in a new direction while momentum moves the aircraft along its old heading. Eventually, the engines' thrust overcomes momentum and establishes the new heading. The difference between the aircraft's heading (where the nose is pointing) and where momentum pushes it is the AOA.

Why Is AOA Important?

Understanding AOA is critical to air combat. AOA, not speed, determines when an aircraft stalls. Regardless of how fast you're going, if the AOA increases enough to disrupt airflow over the wings, the aircraft will stall. Because of this, you may think that you should try to minimize AOA at all times; but of course, there's a catch.

Lift increases as AOA and airspeed increase. As long as you don't exceed stall AOA, the more AOA you pull the more lift you pull. Why is that important? Lift is the same as *G-load*, the force that blacks-out pilots, bends wings, breaks airplanes, but also improves turn performance. I won't reiterate the math involved; just remember: When G-load increases, turn rate increases and turn radius decreases. Therefore, pulling higher AOA results in higher G, resulting in better turn performance. That's the catch—*this* particular aspect implies that you should try to maximize AOA. Increasing AOA improves turn performance, but increasing past stall AOA stalls the aircraft and devastates turn performance. The trick during a dogfight, then, is to fly the aircraft to the "edge of the envelope"—at the maximum AOA possible without stalling it.

This is not as easy as it sounds. It requires finesse and precision under difficult and demanding circumstances. When the aircraft stalls, the rough airflow over the wings causes the whole aircraft to vibrate, or *buffet*. Some aircraft buffet violently in the stall, others vibrate violently before the stall. Some aircraft buffet only during deep stalls. Most aircraft develop a very slight

> If the aircraft buffets, you've probably already pulled too far.

vibration, called the *tickle*, at maximum AOA. Experienced pilots find that tickle and stick to it. Pulling even slightly beyond the tickle has devastating results. This simulated Su-27 offers few physical AOA cues. Generally, the aircraft will develop a slight buffet just at the edge of the stall. In general, if you feel buffet, you've pulled too much!

What Happens During a Stall?

What exactly happens during a stall and why is it bad? When the aircraft stalls, the wings produce little or no lift. We just determined that increasing lift increases turn performance. Likewise, reducing lift reduces turn performance. Stalling, or reducing lift to near-zero, devastates turn performance. Try flying a tight circle over a building (or other fixed ground object). Looking down your wing at the object, it appears to rotate beneath you as you turn. When you stall, however, the aircraft stops turning and moves in a straight-line tangent to the original turn circle. When this happens, the house appears to slide in a straight line away from you.

When you stall, your opponent can gain position behind you. While stalled, you have little control over a conventional aircraft. To regain control, you must reduce AOA below stall AOA. During all of this, the bandit maneuvers behind you. The key, therefore, is remaining right at maximum AOA without exceeding it and stalling! In essence, stalls are nature's way of punishing a pilot for demanding too much from his aircraft.

Spins and Departures

So, what are spins? If you push an aircraft too far into a stall, bad things called *departures* (short for "departure from controlled flight") occur. As the name implies, "departures from controlled flight" mean the pilot no longer controls the aircraft. It's floundering around the sky according to the laws of aerodynamics and the pilot is merely along for the ride. Spins, therefore, are a type of departure.

Spins occur when a stall is coupled with high yaw rates. Perhaps the pilot steps too hard on the rudder; perhaps the aircraft loses an engine; perhaps gravity slices the nose down. Any of these events cause *yaw*, or a sideways motion of the nose. Couple that motion with a stall AOA and you get a departure.

If stalls are nature's way of punishing the pilot for pushing the aircraft too far, a *spin* is nature torturing the pilot for going well beyond the limits. The

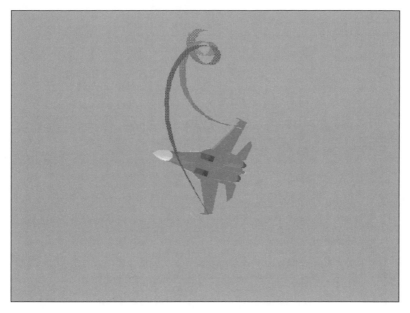

Figure 2-6 A typical spin viewed from below the aircraft.

pilot stays at the edge of a stall during most of a dogfight anyway. The urge to pull "just a little more" performance out of the aircraft is often irresistible. The result—a very high stall probability. The more stalls you enter, the more likely one of them will develop into a spin. Hence the phrase, "edge of the envelope." The combat pilot pushes the aircraft to the very edge of the flight envelope and is punished if he pushes it any further.

> Spins killed thousands of pilots in WWI before they understood what a spin was and how to recover from it. Learn the recovery procedures or share their fate.

Upright Spin Entry and Recovery

Because you spend most of your combat time skirting the edge of a spin or departure, you must know how to recover from them in case one does occur. Figure 2-6 shows a typical spin viewed from below the aircraft. The wingtip smoke trails indicate the aircraft's corkscrew flight path. You can practice spin entry with the following procedure:

Upright Spin Entry Checklist

❑ 1. Climb to 10,000 meters.

❑ 2. Pitch the aircraft up approximately 75 degrees.

❑ 3. Cut the throttle.

❑ 4. When the aircraft stalls, the nose will begin to drop. When the nose drops, apply full rudder (in either direction).

❑ 5. Hold rudder input until the nose has passed through the horizon. By this time you should have entered an upright spin.

During a spin, you're just along for the ride. You can't steer the plane or fight. Plus, the aircraft is losing altitude rapidly in the spin. A typical spin can easily consume 3,000 meters of altitude before recovery. Recovery procedures are fairly simple:

Spin Recovery Checklist

❑ 1. Reduce throttles to idle power.

❑ 2. Center the stick laterally. Apply a slight nose-down attitude.

❑ 3. Apply rudder opposite to the direction of the spin.

❑ 4. When rotation stops apply power and climb out.

This standard spin recovery procedure works on the vast majority of the world's aircraft. Why reduce power? Contrary to popular myth, airspeed has nothing to do with spin recovery. Higher power settings cause the aircraft to dive faster. Lower power helps slow the aircraft and reduces any torque contributing to the yawing motion. The key to spin recovery is to *reduce the yaw, then recover from the stall.*

Applying rudder opposite the spin reduces yaw and eventually straightens the aircraft out. Determining the spin direction can be difficult, however. First, the very nature of a spin is some-what disorienting. Second, the computer can't convey as much physical information to the simulation pilot as a real aircraft conveys to its pilot. Third, older computers with slow frame rates may not update the screen often enough to determine which way the aircraft is spinning. The simple solution: look at the turn-and-slip indicator and apply rudder opposite to the floating ball. If the ball slides right, apply left rudder and vice versa.

Trust the turn-and-slip indicator. It doesn't lie.

Inverted Spins

Figure 2-7 shows an inverted spin. It's basically the same as an upright spin; however, the aircraft is upside down during the spin instead of right-side up. Inverted spins tend to be more disorienting than upright spins, making it harder to determine direction of rotation.

To enter an inverted spin, follow the procedure for an upright spin. After pitching up 75 degrees in step 2, roll the aircraft inverted. When the spin develops, the aircraft will be upside down. Use the same recovery

Figure 2-7 The inverted spin

procedure outline for upright spins. Contrary to popular myth, *always apply rudder opposite the direction of rotation*, regardless of whether upright or inverted. As usual, trust the turn-and-slip indicator; it accurately indicates the direction of rotation regardless whether it's upright or inverted.

Departure Conclusion

The combat pilot spends a good deal of time skirting stalls and spins, increasing the likelihood of unintentionally entering a departure. It is imperative that you understand spin recovery procedures *before* experiencing one in combat.

CHAPTER THREE

Avionics

Su-27 Flanker offers a complex, realistic portrayal of the Su-27's avionics suite. HUD modes, displays, and operational details accurately reflect real-world Su-27 systems. You may find the avionics suite somewhat cumbersome. Navigational information only becomes available when you use navigational HUD modes, switching radar modes often resets weapons and target locks, and the radar is sometimes quite difficult to lock onto target. These are realistic limitations found in the real aircraft that *Su-27* accurately portrays. The aircraft has been criticized for its pilot-intensive cockpit workload. Unlike Western designs that attempt to minimize pilot workload, the Su-27 places a heavy burden on the pilot.

The problem, of course, is finding information. Each HUD/radar mode is designed to present specific information to the pilot. However, considering the six HUD modes contain numerous "submodes," depending on the task, finding the correct HUD for the current situation is a formidable task.

You need not memorize exact HUD modes and the keystrokes required to active them. Instead, you will logically arrive at any desired HUD mode simply by the way you organize the information provided by the individual modes. First, mentally categorize the HUD modes into three groups—navigation, air-to-air, and air-to-ground. Next, remember the data each mode presents. Third, remember how to shift submodes. This procedure permits you to identify logically the type of data you need, where to find it, and how to access it without memorizing long lists of keyboard commands. This could be an *object-oriented* approach using logic and organization to find data, much as object-oriented programming relies on logic and organization to access data items.

Navigational HUD Modes

Basically, the navigational avionics modes get you "from here to there." You have no inflight map available; you must rely on the navigational HUD mode to find your route to the target and home again. Accessed by pressing the ⒈ key, the navigational mode has four sub modes.

When you need navigation or flight attitude information, press ⒈ to select Navigational Modes.

Nav Submode

The **HAB** (*nav*) mode is generally useless to the simulation pilot. Real-world pilots practice "dead reckoning" navigation, using only a compass and a stop watch. In the real world, pilots may fly over large areas, such as an ocean or Siberia, where no radio navaids are available. Under those circumstances, dead reckoning skills are a must. The **HAB** HUD submode provides a relatively clean HUD for this purpose.

In this simulation, however, it is rare that you'll be called on to dead-reckon your way across the battlefield unless your HUD is damaged and you can't access a better navigational mode. Of course, if your HUD is damaged, you won't be able to access this particular mode either. In general, this mode provides little benefit to the simulation player; however, it always appears as the default submode whenever you select a "navigational" HUD mode.

Information Provided: Basically, this mode shows your flight attitude: where the plane is pointed, how high it is, and how fast it's going.

When to Use: Some weapon modes do not provide pitch and bank information on the HUD. Switch to this mode when you've become disoriented

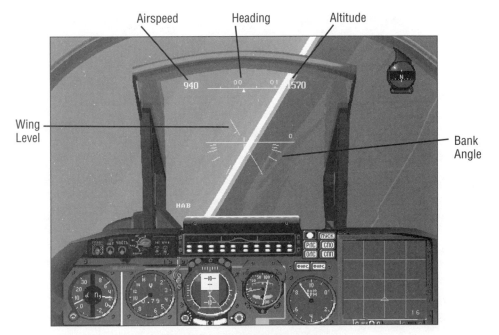

Figure 3-1 Nav mode shows basic flight orientation.

during a dogfight, especially if the nose is pitched so high or low that you cannot see the horizon.

Marsh Submode

The **МАРШ** (*marsh*) mode is the primary navigational mode. Select it by pressing (Caps Lock) once after selecting the navigational HUD. This mode details where your waypoints lie and how you get to them. Generally, you switch to this mode to locate the next waypoint, set the appropriate course, then switch back to an appropriate weapons mode.

In this mode, the MFD provides the only map available during flight. Interestingly, however, the HUD indicates the exact speed and altitude required to reach the waypoint. The floating circle indicates where the waypoint actually exists in space. If you put the circle in the center of the HUD, you'll fly directly to the waypoint. Quite simply, you just "fly through the hoops."

Note also that the ADI includes required bank, heading, and pitch needles. As described on page 41 of the manual, these needles also guide you to

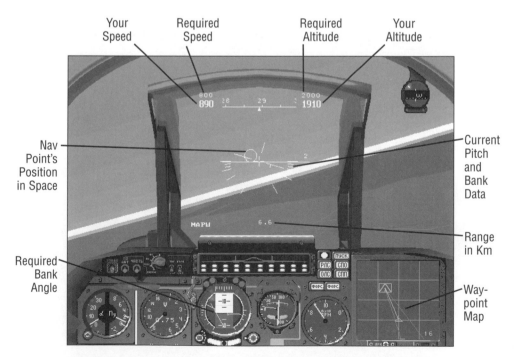

Figure 3-2 The Marsh HUD provides a wealth of information.

the next waypoint. This indicator is especially useful if the HUD is destroyed in combat.

Information Provided: Location of individual waypoints along with a map of all waypoints available on the MFD.

When to Use: Anytime you need to set your course. In general, switch to this mode, set course, then switch to a more appropriate combat mode. Occasionally switch back to this mode to verify course and position.

Vozv Submode

The **BO3B** (*vozv*) mode guides you toward the nearest airport. Instead of taking you directly to the airport, however, the Vozv mode guides to you the *initial approach fix* or IAF, the point in space where you intercept the ILS and begin your approach. The IAF provides sufficient distance from the runway for a normal landing approach. I strongly recommend you begin all landings by flying to the IAF, especially during emergencies. This ensures you sufficient

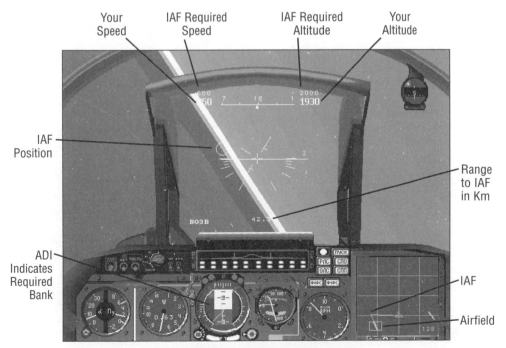

Figure 3-3 Vozv mode prepares you for a good landing.

time to establish a viable approach. If you cut corners on the landing approach, your landings will suffer and possibly result in a crash.

Also called "return mode," this mode also initiates the automatic landing sequence. First, activate the autopilot, then select the Vozv mode. The aircraft will fly to the IAF, intercept the ILS beacon, and automatically land itself.

Information Provided: Location of the IAF for the nearest airfield.

When to Use: Anytime you need to land without following your waypoints all the way home. Also, activating the autopilot, then selecting Vozv mode, initiates an *automatic* landing.

Pos Submode

The **ПОС** (*pos*) mode, the "landing" mode, provides all information required during final approach and landing, including the ILS lines and vertical velocity displayed on the HUD. When selected manually, the Pos mode points directly to the nearest runway. The Pos mode is selected automatically when the aircraft, using Vozv mode, flies to the IAF.

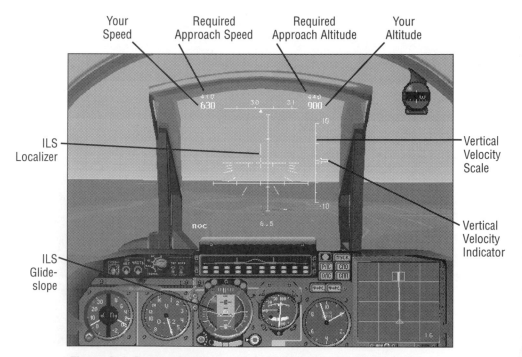

Figure 3-4 Pos mode guides you from the IAF to the runway.

Information Provided: Landing aids.

When to Use: During final approach on any landing. Selected automatically when the aircraft uses Vozv to reach the IAF.

Conclusion

You need not memorize how many times you must press [Caps Lock] to reach any given navigational submode. Just remember two things: 1) press [1] to enter navigation mode; 2) press [Caps Lock] until you find the appropriate submode.

Air-to-Air

The large number of air-to-air HUD modes indicates the Su-27's emphasis on air-to-air combat. The Su-27 has four main air-to-air combat modes: **ДВБ** (*dvb*) for long-range combat; **БВБ** (*bvb*) for visual-range combat; **ШЛЕМ** (*shlem*) for high-aspect dogfights; and **ФИО** (*fio*) for directional missile launches. Each mode's HUD display distinguishes missiles from guns.

Obviously, the more modes you master, the better Su-27 pilot you'll be. On the average, however, it's not necessary to use every air-to-air HUD mode. This section presents the advantages and disadvantages of each mode. Select one long-range and one short-range mode to become proficient with. Once you master those two modes, then you can worry about the other systems. I suggest you begin with **ДВБ** and **БВБ** modes, then explore the **ШЛЕМ** mode, and last the **ФИО** mode.

Dvb Submode

The **ДВБ** (*dvb*) submode is your primary, long-range search mode as well as your primary long-range attack mode. AWACS datalinks the overall radar picture directly to your MFD, but if AWACS isn't available you must rely on Dvb mode to detect enemy aircraft. The system is slaved to either the radar or EOS (using EOS significantly reduces maximum search range, obviously).

The Dvb submode isn't a particularly easy-to-understand system. I can't help wondering why Soviet designers created this particular system, especially when it uses available display space to reiterate the same information twice instead of providing additional targeting data. Nonetheless, SSI seems to have created an accurate simulation.

Searching for Targets

First, detected targets appear both on the MFD and the HUD. *Both MFD and HUD show top-down displays.* This is very important: A target shown at the top of the HUD is farther from your aircraft than a target displayed at the bottom of the HUD. The MFD always shows the target relative to your aircraft. If the target is shown left of center, it is left of your aircraft. On the HUD, however, the target designator (TD) box is referenced to the center of the radar scan. If you move the radar scan to the left or right, the targets on the HUD move accordingly. Figure 3-5 illustrates.

Note that the MFD shows the target directly ahead of the Su-27, but the HUD shows the TD box on the far left. Why? Because the radar scan is deflected to the right. The target, which is in front of the aircraft, is positioned to the left of the radar scan. Therefore, the HUD shows the TD box to the left, indicating you need to move the radar scan to the left to center it on the target.

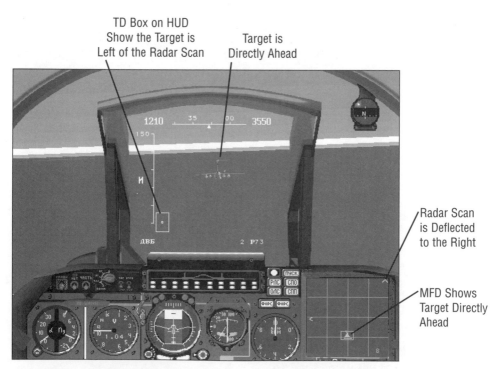

Figure 3-5 The TD box on the HUD is referenced to the radar scan.

Tracking Targets

Dvb mode can track a single target. The radar, however, can't track other targets while locked onto a single bandit. Unless AWACS provides a datalink, only the locked target will appear on the MFD. All other targets will "disappear." Note that Dvb mode contains very little flight attitude information. The HUD is reduced simply to long-range, multi-target scans.

Figure 3-6 shows a Dvb HUD in tracking mode. Note that this photo was staged at extremely close range to illustrate a few points. Typically, you'd use this HUD mode against targets 15 to 20 km away. Referring to figure 3-6, let's examine the Dvb tracking HUD in detail:

1. *The Target Heading Indicator* in the lower left corner rotates to show which way the target is heading relative to your heading. This provides a graphical representation of the aspect angle between the two aircraft. In general, the lower the aspect angle (the more closely the target's flight path matches yours), the more likely your weapons will hit the target.

2. The vertical bar on the left side of the HUD represents the selected weapons range. The number at the top represents the length of the scale (5 km in this

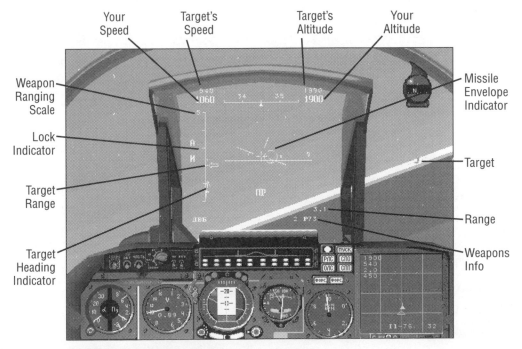

Figure 3-6 Dvb mode HUD tracking a target.

case). Horizontal hash marks on the left side of the line represent 20 percent of the total range (1 km per mark, in this example). Horizontal marks on the right side of the scale represent weapons range. If there is only one mark, it represents the weapon's minimum launch distance. If there are two marks, the lower mark represents the minimum launch distance and the upper mark represents the weapon's maximum range. The arrow floats up and down the right side of the scale, indicating target distance.

3. *The Lock Indicator* (the 'A' symbol on the far left) indicates when you've locked onto a target (as if you couldn't tell from the rest of the HUD!).

4. The target's speed and altitude are listed along the top of the HUD, above your own speed and altitude readings.

5. The circle in the center of the HUD represents the missile's launch envelope. The small box, or target indicator, must be inside the circle when you launch or the missile will miss. In this example, the target is too far outside the envelope circle.

6. Looking down to the MFD, you'll see the data block in the upper left corner of the MFD lists target altitude, airspeed, range, and closure rate. The closure rate is the relative speed between you and your target. You can visualize this several ways:

   - It's the difference in speed between you and your target. If it is positive, you are getting closer. If it is negative, you are getting farther apart.

   - It's the speed you would fly if the target were a stationary object. If the target suddenly stopped moving, you would have to fly (in this example) 540 km/hr to approach the target at the same rate.

   - Technically (and most accurately), it's the mathematical addition of your velocity vector and the target's velocity vector. Accordingly, closure rate varies as the angle between your heading and the target's heading varies. A closure rate of zero indicates you are getting no closer to (or farther away from) the target; you are maintaining a consistent range.

Once you understand all the indicators, using the Dvb HUD for long-range intercepts is fairly easy and follows a simple procedure:

1. Manipulate the radar scan until you detect targets.

2. Lock onto an individual target.

3. Close on the target until the range indicator drops below your weapon's maximum range mark on the ranging scale.

4. Maneuver until the target indicator comes inside the missile envelope circle. Note: The intercept geometry often dictates that you do not maneuver inside the missile envelope until you close within range and reduce aspect angle as much as possible.

5. Fire your weapon.

Information Provided: Long-range scanning of multiple targets, long-range tracking of a single target, long-range missile-launch information.

When to Use: When searching for targets at long range, especially when AWACS is unavailable. Also, when intercepting targets with missiles at long range.

Bvb Submode

Dvb submode works well for long-ranged intercepts, but once you're in dogfight range you need flight attitude data back on the HUD. The **БВБ** (*bvb*) submode shown in figure 3-7 provides a combination of weapons, target, and flight attitude information.

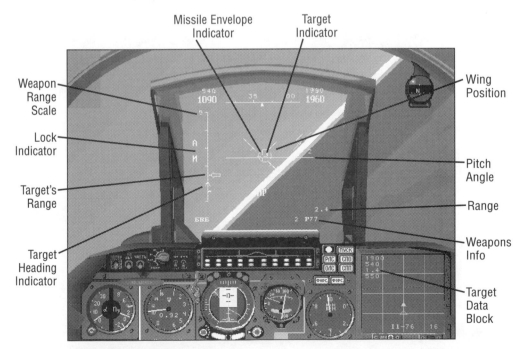

Figure 3-7 Bvb mode HUD

For the most part, when locked onto a target, Bvb uses the same indicators as Dvb mode. When not locked onto a target, however, Bvb mode does *not* show target indicators on the HUD. Refer to the Dvb section for a detailed explanation of the various HUD indicators.

Information Provided: Flight attitude data, tracking data for a single target.

When to Use: When the flight transitions inside 25 km.

Shlem Submode

The ШЛЕМ (*shlem*) submode together with advanced, off-boresight missiles gives the Flanker pilot an extra punch during a knife fight. Anyone who's experienced a close-range dogfight knows the pilot spends quite a bit of time looking through the top of the canopy at a target he can't quite bring the nose onto. Conventional missiles can't fire at a target more than 10 or 20 degrees off the aircraft's nose.

The Russian R-73 (AA-11) provides up to 60 degrees of off-boresight launch capability. In other words, if the target is within a 60-degree cone of the aircraft's nose, the pilot can launch a missile at it. Of course, the pilot must be able to obtain a lock on the target, so his helmet comes equipped with a targeting sight. By turning his head, he can lock onto the target and fire a missile even though the target may be well outside the HUD. The USAF ran a series of simulations comparing the volume of space within which a target could be locked onto between a MiG-29 (which uses the same radar, R-73s, and Shlem system as the Su-27) and an F-15 (equipped with AIM-9Ms). The simulation found the MiG could acquire targets in a volume 30 times larger than the F-15 could.

Shlem mode *is not* the end-all of air combat. It doesn't make the Su-27 an invincible, super dogfighter. First, only the R-73 missile offers off-boresight capability. Second, as stated above, the system supports only 60 degrees off-boresight, not 180 degrees. In other words, you still must press an offensive advantage to exploit the

> The R-73, using Shlem mode, can lock onto targets up to 60 degrees off your nose. If the target is any farther off your nose, the missile can't acquire the target.

Figure 3-8 Shlem mode looking forward.

60-degree capability. If you're neutral (target is 90 degrees off your nose) or defensive (target is 91 to 180 degrees off your nose), the Shlem system can't help you. *You must be able to dogfight your aircraft to exploit Shlem mode.*

You'll note from Figure 3-8 that Shlem mode looking directly forward is almost identical to the Bvb HUD except for the Shlem aiming circle. Figure 3-9 shows the view when Shlem looks outside the HUD. When you move the view far enough that the HUD is not visible, the Shlem sight adds a "flight attitude" display beneath the aiming reticle. Note from the HUD in figure 3-9 that the target designator is well outside the missile envelope circle. This is normal for Shlem shots using the R-73.

In reality, 60 degrees off-boresight is probably less than it seems. To see for yourself, try creating a new mission. Place a friendly IL-76 on a long, slow patrol. Practice intercepting the IL-76 using the Shlem system. Approach the target along a parallel course about 2 km to one side. Press the [*] key to pad-lock the target. The Shlem view will naturally slide with padlock to maintain the target and slowly overtake the jet. Observe your exact location when the Shlem finally breaks lock.

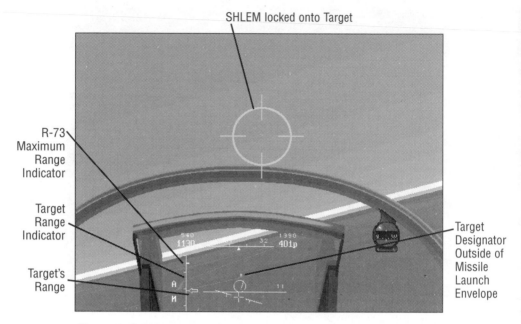

SHLEM locked onto Target

R-73
Maximum
Range
Indicator

Target
Range
Indicator

Target's
Range

Target
Designator
Outside of
Missile
Launch
Envelope

Figure 3-9 Shlem mode looking out the canopy.

Special Feature

You can use Shlem to guide missile seekers without radar or EOS. Maneuver the target into the Shlem targeting circle, padlock the target, then lock the seeker onto the target. Tracking range and lock angles depend on the gimbal limits of the seeker head, the type of seeker, and the target's size. This tactic is very useful if your radar and EOS have been damaged.

Information Provided: No tracking data, but allows locking onto targets up to 60 degrees off your aircraft's nose.

When to Use: During a tight dogfight when preparing a high-angle R-73 shot.

Fio Submode

ФИО (*fio*) mode lets appropriately equipped missiles lock onto targets without first acquiring a radar or EOS lock on the target. Fio is only useful for *within-visual-range* (WVR) engagements. If the selected missile has an appropriate seeker, a 3-degree targeting circle appears in the center of the HUD. Maneuver the target inside the aiming circle, lock the target, and fire.

Figure 3-10 Fio submode prior to locking the target.

Figure 3-11 Fio submode after acquiring the target. Notice that the aiming circle becomes smaller.

Fio only works for IR-guided missiles (which home in on the heat emitted by the target) and active-radar missiles (that track the target using an onboard radar). Fio won't work with semi-active radar homing (SARH) missiles. SARH missiles home in on radar waves emitted from the launching aircraft and reflected by the target. You can use Fio with the following missiles:

1. R-73 (heat-seeking)

2. R-27T (heat-seeking)

3. R-77 (active radar)

Information Provided: None.

When to Use: To fire a missile at a target within visual range without activating either the radar or EOS (or whenever the radar and EOS have been damaged).

 ## Air-to-Ground Avionics

The Su-27's air-to-ground avionics package is fairly straightforward. How you employ it varies with the selected weapons package, but I'll discuss weapons usage in the next chapter. For now, I'll concentrate on what the **ЗЕМЛЯ** (*zemlya*) mode provides.

Although ground attack is usually classified a "secondary" role for the Su-27, the Flanker carries a very capable ground-mapping radar. In general, attacks follow a simple procedure: Lock onto a ground target with the radar. An indicator appears on the HUD overlaying the locked target. Point the weapons and shoot.

Scan Mode

To lock a ground target, you must select the Zemlya mode *and* activate the radar. The EOS won't lock onto ground targets. Immediately, a ground map produced by the radar appears on the MFD. The range to the mapped area varies depending on your altitude; the higher and faster you fly, the farther forward the ground radar can see. You can move the scan zone forward or backward slightly using the radar scan control keys, but you don't have a whole lot of control. The small diamond on the HUD indicates where the radar is looking. If the area the radar is mapping is not visible in the HUD, a hash mark appears along the closest HUD edge. This particular step is called *Scan mode*.

Figure 3-12 Search Wide Area (SWA) mode

Search Wide Area

Access the *Search Wide Area* (SWA) mode by pressing the ⊕ key while in scan mode. Actually, SWA is a misleading name. SWA provides a higher magnification map than Scan mode and adds a frame to the MFD (shown in figure 3-12). This box is controlled by the radar/EOS scan control keys and chooses an area to focus even more tightly.

As you're flying along, you'll suddenly notice a town, an airfield, or whatever come into the map. Using the scan controls, move the frame over the top of the site, then press the ⊕ key again. This locks the radar to a smaller area.

Search Narrow Area

The *Search Narrow Area* (SNA) mode focuses tightly enough to distinguish individual aircraft, vehicles, and buildings on the ground. Cross hairs (controlled by the radar scan controls) in the MFD indicate precisely where the radar is looking. The HUD diamond moves in correlation, overlaying the designated target. At this point, you merely point the weapons at the diamond and follow appropriate launch procedures.

SNA mode has one particularly important aspect: It remembers the last locked position regardless of your maneuvers. If you fly past that particular

Figure 3-13 Search Narrow Area (SNA) mode

point the radar will lose lock, but will immediately reacquire the *same spot* as soon as you maneuver the location back into your radar's coverage. This feature offers some very useful advantages, especially if your weapons miss the target. If enemy defenses allow, simply leave the radar locked to the target and make a new attack run!

> The SNA remembers the coordinates of the locked ground. If the radar loses lock (because of your maneuvering), the SNA will automatically reacquire the same location as soon as you maneuver that location back into radar coverage.

Conclusion

The Su-27, when used according to its strengths, is a formidable weapons platform by any measure. I suggest you fly a few sample missions with only an unarmed transport aircraft to practice working the air-to-air avionics modes. Likewise, fly a few solo sorties over an airbase and practice picking out targets with the ground radar. Once you've mastered the avionics, it's time to graduate to weapons delivery.

CHAPTER FOUR

Su-27
Tactics

There's more to flying the Su-27 than simply understanding Basic Fighter Maneuvers (BFM). Although BFM, or dogfighting, is a major part of many *Su-27* missions, you also need to know a few tips and tricks with the padlock view system, missile evasion, and avionics usage in addition to dogfighting skills.

Views

Su-27 is one of the first flight simulators that models cockpit view limitations. Some aircraft, such as the F-16, use tall bubble canopies allowing the pilot to lean around and look behind the aircraft. The Su-27, however, recesses the pilot fairly low in the cockpit. The canopy rails, ejection seat, and rear fuselage make it impossible to see directly behind the aircraft. SSI accurately recreated these view limitations. You can't turn your view past the 5 o'clock and 7 o'clock positions and the padlock view loses its lock when the target maneuvers into your blind spot.

Assessing View Limitations

Figures 4-1 and 4-2 illustrate the Su-27's view limitations. Using two Su-27s in close formation can map the exact view limits. Figure 4-1 shows a view to the right. Even when the view rotates completely to the right, you can see only the wingman's nose and front edge of the fuselage numbers.

Figure 4-2 shows the same two aircraft from above. We can easily see how far the wingman's nose is behind the flight leader. The 90-degree line indicates the leader's 3 o'clock position. Further, by drawing a line from the leader's cockpit to the wingman's fuselage numbers, we can measure the maximum viewing angle. From this example, we can determine that the Su-27 pilot can see about 30 degrees behind his 3-9 line (the imaginary line drawn from his 3 o'clock to his 9 o'clock position).

This is the Su-27's primary liability during a dogfight. If the bandit gets in your rear quarter, you *can't* see him. You must always keep the enemy head of your 3-9 line to ensure you can see him and that the padlock view can lock onto him. If the bandit makes it behind you, you have little choice but to continue a maximum performance turn while trying to ascertain where the bandit is. We'll explore this problem in greater detail later.

Figure 4-1 Maximum View Deflection

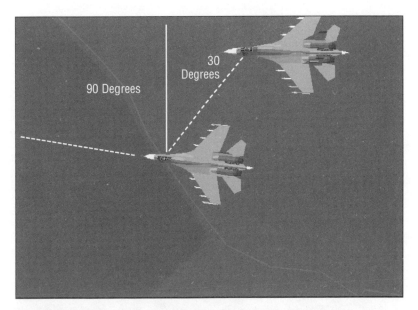

Figure 4-2 Maximum View Deflection awards 30 degrees of view behind the 3-9 line.

Using Padlock

SSI adds a new twist to an old padlock style, converting it from relatively use-less eye candy into an effective combat view. What most simulations call a "padlock view" is merely keeping the bandit visible in the screen. There are no indicators, however, that explain where the user is looking. It's impossible to distinguish between your high 5 o'clock position and your high 1 o'clock position, since no part of your aircraft is visible in the periphery. In the end, you have no idea where you're looking or how to maneuver.

Su-27, however, adds a small HUD-type display to the padlock view. This mini-HUD always stays on the edge of your screen closest to the actual HUD. For example, if the padlock view looks at 9 o'clock high, the mini-HUD stays in the bottom right corner of the screen. If you manually rotate the view toward the mini-HUD, you will always wind up looking at the normal forward view. Figure 4-3 illustrates.

Well-designed padlock view systems make close-range dogfights signifi-cantly easier, allowing the simulation pilot to see what a real-world pilot sees during a dogfight. Padlock views can be extremely disorienting without the proper training and procedures.

Figure 4-3 The mini-HUD always points to the main HUD.

Padlock Training

1. Learn to fly. First and foremost you must learn to fly your aircraft while using the padlock view. The mini-HUD appears whenever the view shifts significantly from the normal forward view, whether the padlock system moved it or you moved it manually. Therefore, manually shift the view to the left until the mini-HUD appears. Continue shifting the view until you can no longer see the main HUD.

Next, forget about the horizon. Do not even look at it. Focus only on the mini-HUD. It shows your airspeed, altitude, pitch and bank angles—everything you need to fly your aircraft. Focusing on the mini-HUD, level the aircraft. Do not change the view or look at the horizon; simply focus on the mini-HUD and move the controls accordingly until you're flying straight and level.

Now, gently bank the aircraft into a turn. At first, try something easy like a 20-degree bank. Focus *only* on the mini-HUD. Use the stick and rudders as necessary to keep the pitch angle at zero while banking 20 degrees. Once you can execute a sustained 20-degree turn, increase the bank angle to 45 degrees and repeat. Last, increase bank angle to 90 degrees and repeat the lesson.

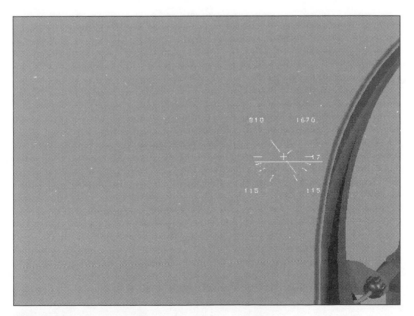

Figure 4-4 The mini-HUD indicates we're looking up and to the left while the aircraft executes a climbing right turn.

When you've mastered turns, practice taking the Su-27 to different altitudes and leveling off using only the mini-HUD. Climb to 8,000 m, level off, descend to 6,000 m, level off, then climb back to 8,000 m.

When you complete that, try this final exam: Create a blank mission with your Su-27 at 6,000 m and choose the Record menu option. Start at 6,000 m. Rotate the view to the right until you can see only the mini-HUD. Now, execute a climbing left turn to 7,500 m. Level out, then descend to 7,000 m. At 7,000 m, execute a descending right turn to 6,000 m. Last, level out, then pitch the nose straight up and execute a loop. End the mission and replay the tape. If you can execute those maneuvers solely by looking at the mini-HUD, you're ready for the next step.

2. Learn to look. You must immediately recognize where the padlock view is looking relative to the nose of your aircraft. Again, rely on the mini-HUD to explain this. Why do you need to know where the bandit is relative to your nose? Because your lift vector (the imaginary line that indicates which way the lift from your wings is pushing your aircraft) extends right out the top of your canopy, perpendicular to your wings. At some point during the dogfight it will become necessary to point your lift vector at the bandit and pull the

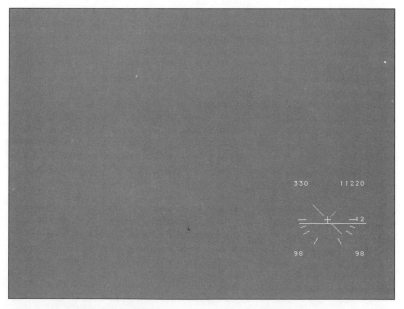

Figure 4-5 The mini HUD always points to the real HUD.

Figure 4-6 Execute aerobatic maneuvers while keeping a friendly aircraft padlocked.

stick back. You must, therefore, know where the bandit is relative to your aircraft so you know where to point the aircraft. Your aircraft's nose makes a convenient reference point.

Practice with other aircraft. Create a new mission. Add a flight of Russian MiG-29s flying a complex, zigzagging path. Add your Su-27 just behind the MiG-29s. When the mission begins, practice padlocking the MiGs and pulling them into the normal forward view. Roll and turn your aircraft so that you lose padlock, then turn your Su-27 until you can reacquire. Then, repeat the exercise and pull the MiGs into your normal forward view. Even with off-boresight missiles, you must still bring your target into your forward quarter before firing. Practice using the padlock against non-maneuvering targets until you can steer the target into your forward view every time.

Next, using the mini-HUD while padlocked onto a MiG, execute a series of aerobatic maneuvers. Execute a barrel roll around the MiG, execute a high yo-yo when the MiG initiates a turn, and even try flying formation with the padlocked MiG. This familiarizes you with the view of a padlocked target and the mini-HUD while flying at unusual attitudes.

The training steps outlined in this section should require no more than a couple of hours of practice time, but will *significantly* improve your dogfighting skills. Resist the urge to immediately start a combat mission and dive in on the enemy. Take the time to learn the padlock system before trying to use it in combat.

Padlock In Combat

Once you are familiar with the padlock system, using it in combat comes down to an easy, multi-step process:

1. Padlock a bandit. Obviously you need to lock the target as soon as possible.

2. Activate Shlem mode. Shlem (and off-boresight missiles) gives you an edge in a dogfight—use it!

3. Pull the mini-HUD toward the bandit. In general, try to get your nose on the bandit and take a shot as soon as possible. When in doubt, *point your nose at the enemy.* If the bandit appears left of the mini-HUD, come left. If the mini-HUD is below the bandit, pull up. Remember, the mini-HUD always resides on the edge of the screen closest to your aircraft's nose. Pulling the mini-HUD toward the bandit pulls your nose toward the bandit.

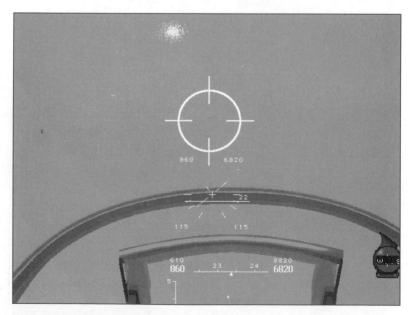

Figure 4-7 Using padlock for a Shlem shot.

Obviously, in some tactical cases you don't want to pull your nose on the bandit. For example, you must pull your nose away to execute a high yo-yo. In general, though, at some point you *must* pull your nose toward the enemy to shoot him.

4. Fire when in parameters. When you get the bandit inside of weapon parameters, shoot!

Working Against the Blind Spot

The biggest problem are the view limitations. If you let the bandit get behind you, you may not see him for the rest of your simulated life! In a dogfight you need to keep the bandit padlocked as much as possible. When tracking a single bandit, real-world combat pilots never take their eyes off the target. Neither should you. Real-world pilots, however, can physically feel the pitch and bank of their aircraft. This physical feedback helps ascertain where the bandit is relative to the attacker's nose. In this simulation you must rely on the mini-HUD for that information.

Missile Evasion

Although most pilots (simulation or otherwise) prefer to boast about their numerous air-to-air kills, if you fly long enough you will inevitably get shot at. When that happens, you must *immediately* know *exactly* what to do. One mistake and the length of your simulated life equals the incoming missile's remaining flight time.

Missile Defense

Generally, you'll get a missile warning indicator whenever a missile heads your way; however, you don't always get the warning until quite some time after the missile has been launched. The missile may be well on its way toward you by the time your warning panel lights up.

Not all missiles require the launching platform to radar lock you. Other Su-27s may track you via AWACS datalink and fire missiles using Fio mode without ever activating their radar. A MiG-29 or Su-27 may track you using the EOS and never betray its presence on your radar warning receiver. If, however, an enemy aircraft or SAM site *does* radar lock you, rest assured they have hostile intentions. Therefore, as soon as someone radar locks you, *take evasive action immediately!* Begin releasing chaff and flares, then execute a hard turn *toward* the attacker to increase the aspect angle between you and the attacker as much as possible as quickly as possible.

The initial Su-27 release contains a bug rendering your ECM gear inoperative. Don't rely on your jammers!

If you get a missile warning, you must execute some serious evasive maneuvers as quickly as possible. First, check your threat warning display and determine where the threat is. Second, turn toward it. Third, release chaff and flares like there's no tomorrow; if you don't, there might not be.

Hopefully, chaff (for radar guided missiles) and flares (for heat-seekers) will spoof the inbound missile, causing it to chase after the decoy. Keep in mind, though, that a missile doesn't have to hit its target to damage it. A missile warhead usually propels shrapnel (or other devices) when it explodes. If a missile determines it's going to miss, it will still detonate when it gets close to the target. Likewise, if a missile chases a burst of chaff and explodes near your aircraft you may still take damage. Therefore, it's imperative that you *get away from your countermeasures.* When you start releasing chaff and flares, don't keep flying in a circle. You'll complete 360 degrees and end up right back in your own countermeasure cloud. If you see your own chaff in front of you while an enemy missile zooms toward you, *break away fast!*

OK, so you've started evasive maneuvers and releasing countermeasures. If the missile was launched from a long distance, you probably have 30 to 45 seconds before impact. The missile warning may not commence until the missile has been in flight, reducing your time to as little as 20 seconds. How can you determine whether the missile has been launched from a long distance? Check the MFD. It will display the bandit if either it has its radar on or you have a datalink to an AWACS. Otherwise, you can't tell unless you actually see the missile's smoke trail arcing toward you.

If it looks like a long-range shot, level off, engage afterburners, fire two or three chaff/flare bursts, then break hard away from the chaff and *climb.* Remember, missile engines don't burn for the entire missile flight. They fire initially, accelerate the missile rapidly, then run out of fuel. The missile, now moving a few thousand km/hr, glides the rest of the way to the target. As with your aircraft, maneuvering reduces speed, further reducing the missile's maneuverability. If you're at the edge of the missile's envelope, it may not be able to stay with you in a zoom climb.

If you can see the missile's smoke trail, you have other options. The missile emits smoke only when the motor is burning. If the smoke trail isn't getting any closer to you, the motor has burnt out and the missile is somewhere between the smoke trail and you. If you see the trail moving toward you (and getting longer), then you know *exactly* where the missile is. In this case, break hard in either direction until the missile is at your 3 o'clock or your 9 o'clock position. Lower the nose and apply afterburner to maintain maximum speed (unless you suspect the incoming missile is IR-guided. Then you should reduce throttle to cut your heat emissions).

Begin a gentle turn keeping the missile off your wing as it veers toward you. Don't pull too hard at first. Save your energy until the missile gets closer, then yank the stick as hard as you can into your lap. Keep releasing countermeasures, then (while still pulling the stick) roll the wings level and pull up or roll inverted and execute a split S. Keeping the missile off your wing forces it to bleed energy en route; pulling hard as it closes forces it to bleed more energy; chaff and flares give it decoys to sort out, and the break up or down takes you away from the chaff/flare as quickly as possible and forces the missile to maneuver harder.

Run Like a Reptile

If the enemy comes from behind, your best bet may be to run like a reptile. Go to full burner, nose down, and blast away at top speed until you're outside of missile range. You'll find this tactic especially useful against slower aircraft, like the MiG-23. Once you're outside of missile range, depending on the bandit's mission goals, they often lose interest in escaping targets and break off the attack. You can then bug out and head for home or continue with the mission at your discretion.

The Best Defense Is a Good Offense

Missile evasion is a difficult task. Even if you evade the first missile, you've probably used all your energy and don't have enough smash to outmaneuver the inevitable second missile. Your best bet is never letting the enemy take a shot at you in the first place. You have several resources available for this task.

AWACS—Don't Leave Home Without It

First, *never* undertake a mission without an AWACS on station. The datalink will keep you informed of the entire airborne battlefield. With an AWACS airborne there's no legitimate reason for an enemy aircraft getting inside 120 km without being painted on your MFD, unless you simply fail to pay attention. This lets you evade enemy aircraft before they enter firing range.

Fighter Cover

We'll talk more about deploying fighter cover in the Chapter 5, but in general, try to send a group of fighters ahead of the main strike package to thin out enemy fighters ahead of time. Station a series of fighters on patrols crossing each major threat axis. That is, if you know there's an enemy airbase at heading 010, place a pair of fighters on patrol between you and that airbase. The goal is twofold: First, never let the enemy get within firing range undetected. Second, have plenty of assets to counterengage the enemy with. He can't effectively shoot at you if he's already dancing with several friendly missiles.

Turn to Engage

Your primary objective always drives the mission. It doesn't do much good, however, to focus on the objective so much that the enemy blind-sides you. Generally, you need to define an "engagement bubble" around your aircraft. The bubble is based on your air-to-air weapons range, the enemy's air-to-air weapons range, and the goals of your mission. 100 km makes a decent bubble. If the enemy gets closer than 100 km and there's no sign any other friendly units (aircraft or SAMs) will attack it, turn and engage it yourself.

Regardless of what distance you choose, positively identify the engagement bubble *before* you launch the mission. You have to make hundreds of instant decisions in the cockpit, save yourself some tension and make as many decisions as you can while still on the ground.

Carry Long-Range Weapons

Assuming mission priorities permit, carry R-77 long-range missiles as often as possible and don't hesitate to fire them at the enemy at maximum range. As the missile envelope diagram on page 59 of the manual illustrates, you can fire a weapon at longer ranges if the target heads toward you instead of away from you. Missiles in *Su-27* tend to do the most damage when they strike the target in the front quarter, anyway. When possible, give the enemy a missile in his teeth.

Conclusion

Missile evasion skills can make or break a mission. They spell the difference between the thrill of victory and the frustrating agony of defeat. You'll learn missile evasion skills only one way: practice, practice, practice, and practice some more. Timing is more important than the actual maneuvers. A perfect maneuver performed too early will leave you sitting a duck; a sloppy maneuver at the correct instant will keep you alive.

Avionics Usage in Combat

Although cited as a major weakness, the Su-27's dependence on an AWACS datalink for battlefield awareness can be a major strength under the appropriate conditions. Although severely blinded when the AWACS is missing, the Su-27 can perform a stealth fighter imitation when the AWACS is available.

Using Radar/EOS

There's no good reason not to use the electro-optical system. The EOS is purely passive, meaning it emits no radiation of any kind. It merely looks for emissions from other objects. Short-ranged, compared to the radar, it provides significantly more information than having all sensors disabled. Therefore, activate the EOS as soon as your wheels clear the tarmac and keep it on for the whole mission. Its effective range is a little greater than its visual range, making EOS extremely useful during close-range dogfights, although it can't provide detailed information such as range to the target and target speed.

The radar, however, is a different story. It broadcast radar waves, then listens for reflections off objects. Although it's an extremely effective detection device, broadcasting radar waves announces your presence to the entire world. Anyone who cares to listen to the appropriate frequency will know which direction you are. Further, they may be able to identify your aircraft type based on the kind of radar waves you're emitting, and they may even determine your approximate distance by measuring the strength of the received waves and comparing it to your radar output power. Enemies operating the same equipment as you (or who have a thorough intelligence network) can glean a lot of information about you by listening to your radar emissions.

You've probably noticed that in air-to-air combat modes your MFD displays active radar sources, giving you an indication of your enemy's location. If you've lost sight in a dogfight, this might be your only method of relocating the bandit. Unfortunately, this system works both ways. The bandit has similar sensing devices in his cockpit. Therefore, it behooves you to limit your radar use.

First, rely on AWACS for long-range searches. It has a longer range and wider coverage than your onboard radar anyway. With your radar off, you may even be able to sneak up behind the enemy and blast them out of the sky before they know what hit them. Second, once you enter a tight dogfight use only the EOS. The EOS is highly effective at close range; although it can't provide as much data as the radar, it provides *enough* data to launch an R-77 or any heat-seeking missile. Third, don't forget about Fio mode. As I pointed out in Chapter 3, this mode lets you fire heat-seeking and active-radar-homing missiles without activating *any* of your onboard sensors. Fio mode has an extremely restricted engagement envelope, especially when compared to Shlem mode, but it is a very effective stealth system. Fio also comes in useful if your onboard radar suffers battle damage.

Shlem In a Dogfight

Once you enter a close-range dogfight, there's absolutely no reason to not use the Shlem mode. Generally, padlock the bandit first, activate the Shlem mode, then pull the bandit into the engagement envelope and shoot. In the Su-27, you should fly most knife fights using the padlock view mode and the Shlem HUD mode.

Further, as shown in figure 4-8, Shlem mode can use a missile's guidance system to acquire a target off boresight like an expanded Fio mode. Notice the Shlem aiming circle is missing in figure 4-8 because it is flashing to indicate the missile lock. As with Fio, this will only work with heat-seeking or active-radar-homing missiles.

Get the First Shot

Shlem mode gives you two primary dogfighting advantages—first-shot and across-the-circle capabilities. As the name implies, first shot capability means you usually fire the first weapons when a dogfight begins. This capability is fleeting, and first-shot missiles often miss, but it gives you an opportunity to put the enemy on the defensive before the fight really begins. Across-the-cir-

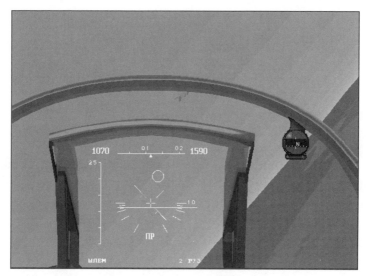

Figure 4-8 SHLEM can lock targets like Fio mode.

cle capability refers to off-boresight missile shots, letting you engage a target up to 60 degrees of your nose. As I mentioned in Chapter 3, this capability does not make you invincible, but it lets you turn a predominately neutral situation into an offensive advantage.

Never underestimate the value of the first shot. Firing first surprises the enemy, forces him to change his game plan and react, can demoralize the opponent, and has a good chance of securing an offensive advantage immediately. When you enter a dogfight, don't wait for a perfect shot. Take any shot opportunity awards.

Front-Quarter Shots Are More Deadly

Repeated experiments in *Su-27* show a consistent result: Missiles do significantly more damage when they strike the target from the front quarter than from the rear. This effect is especially noticeable with twin-engine aircraft. A missile strike to the rear quarter of a twin-engine aircraft usually does substantial damage (often killing one engine), but the target usually remains airworthy. A missile strike to the front quarter nearly always sends the aircraft down in flames. Front-quarter missile strikes are generally more devastating to your Su-27, as well. Therefore, fire into the enemy's face when possible— while trying to avoid taking a shot in your own teeth.

BVR Fight

We've talked about several items applicable to long-range, or beyond-visual-range (BVR), combat. Now let's put the whole puzzle together.

Poles

Suppose you're about to fire an R-77 at a maneuvering target just barely inside the missile's maximum range. What are the odds the missile will strike the target? We measure missile engagement performance in terms of three poles.

F-Pole

The F-pole is the primary measure of missile range, or standoff distance. When two aircraft charge headlong at each other, the one with the longest missile F-pole generally wins. The F-pole provides two useful statistics—how far the missile will go, and who will win an SARH missile joust.

The F-pole is based on the missile's performance specifications, but varies based on the launching platform's speed. Remember that the missile's motor doesn't burn for the entire flight. It accelerates the missile to maximum speed, then runs out of fuel and shuts off. Increasing launch speed imparts more kinetic energy into the missile, causing it to reach maximum speed sooner and retain speed longer. Increasing launch speed, therefore, extends the missile's F-pole and range. If you must hit a target at the maximum edge of your missile's envelope, accelerate as much as possible before launching the weapon.

The F-pole also provides a relative performance measure between two forward-quarter missile shots. Suppose you detect an enemy Su-27 on your nose about 50 km out. You both fire SARH missiles at approximately the same time. Now, both of you must continue to fly toward the target and maintain radar lock until each missile strikes a target. The missile that strikes first will most likely kill the other's radar, causing the associated missile to lose guidance. Which missile will strike first? The missile with the longest F-pole. This situation can be called an SARH missile joust: Both parties charge forward maintaining a radar lock until one missile strikes.

Even if you know the type of aircraft you're facing, you rarely know what flavor of missile the bandit is carrying until after it hits you. Accordingly, you usually can't be certain that your missile's F-pole is longer than the bandit's (unless you know the bandit can't carry long-range weapons). Therefore,

always try to increase your F-pole while
simultaneously shortening the bandit's.
That means increasing speed as much as
possible until you launch your missile, then
slowing down or turning away from the target. Of course, if you're using SARH missiles you must remain within allowable
steering error (ASE). ASE simply means, if you turn too far from the target
you'll lose radar lock and waste the missile.

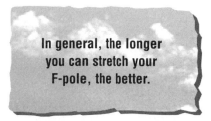

In general, the longer
you can stretch your
F-pole, the better.

A-Pole

The A-pole is to active radar missiles as the F-pole is to SARH missiles.
Instead of indicating when the missile will strike, the A-pole indicates when
the missile will go *active*. Most active radar missiles do not activate their radar
until well after launch. Some, like the AIM-54 Phoenix, fly in SARH mode
to a predetermined distance from the target, then activate their onboard
radar. Others, like the AIM-120 AMRAAM, fly to a preprogramed point in
space using inertial guidance, then activates its onboard radar.

E-Pole

The E-pole describes a "no escape" zone. For example, a hypothetical missile
may specify that if it flies 25 km it *will* strike the target even if the target pulls
an 8 g maneuver at 1,000 km/hr. However, when extended to 35 km it may
only be able to strike a target pulling 5 g or less. The E-pole is an extremely
useful measure allowing you to judge the effectiveness of your missile shot.
Unfortunately, this level of information is generally highly classified and not
publicly available.

Acquiring Position

Air Combat Maneuvering (ACM) refers to the initial jockeying for position
before the fighters actually commence dogfighting. Obviously, killing the
enemy at long range is preferred, especially if he never sees you prior to the
attack. When a dogfight is destined to ensue, however, you must secure an
advantageous position *before* the dogfight commences.

Setting up the *merge*, or the point where the dogfight begins, is one of the
most difficult tasks in air combat, especially in a missile environment. In a
guns-only fight, at least you know the enemy can't have much more than a

fleeting shot as you scream past each other. When missiles enter the picture, however, the front-quarter missile strike makes initial positioning as potentially deadly as the actual dogfight.

Fight Categories

Generally speaking, if the enemy points his nose at you, you're defensive. If you point your nose at the enemy, you're offensive. If neither points at the other, the fight is neutral. While this obviously oversimplifies the situation, it provides a useful context for the following discussion.

Getting Angles

Ideally you should start a fight as offensively as possible. That means having your nose pointed at the enemy, his nose *not* pointed at you, and preferably be approaching his rear quarter from a low aspect angle.

   If the enemy doesn't point his nose at you, you have the option of slowly and methodically maneuvering behind him. This tactic is especially useful if you have an AWACS datalink and you don't betray your position by using your onboard radar. As you might expect, opportunities like this rarely hap-

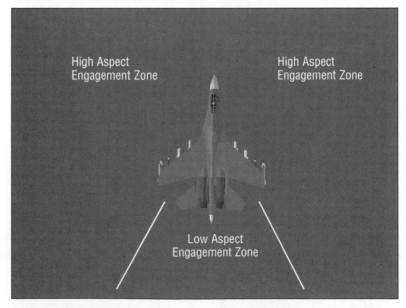

Figure 4-9 High and Low Aspect Engagement Zones

pen. The enemy usually has ground-based radar active; rarely can you maneuver into engagement range inside enemy territory without being detected.

Barrage Tactics

What do you do when the ideal situation isn't an option (that is, most of the time)? A typical, Soviet-era missile barrage is one good way to start the fight, depending on the ordnance you have available. The theory is almost elegant in simplicity: Fire a wall of missiles at the bad guy before he shoots at you. While the bandit tries to evade the inbound missiles, you can either maneuver behind him and finish him off with a close-range shot or bug out and let a second wave of fighters finish him off. The bandit depletes his energy status and probably loses track of you, leaving him a sitting duck even if he manages to evade your barrage.

The tactic works well with active-radar missiles but is less viable with SARH missiles. Once you fire a volley of active-radar missiles, such as the R-77, you can break away from the attack. You can withdraw out of return-fire range or press the attack at your discretion. With SARH missiles, however, you must maintain the radar lock on the target until the missile hits. As described above, in this situation your missile's F-pole must be longer than the enemy's. Otherwise, the enemy's missile will hit you, probably destroy your radar, causing your missile to lose guidance, while the bandit heads for home.

Horizontal or Vertical?

The next question is, "What if I don't have any long-range missiles?" Assuming the bandit *does not* employ barrage tactics against you, you're looking at a classic merge situation. You'll close to visual range, probably pass each other, and then plunge into a dogfight. What should you think about as you enter the fight?

The more you know about the enemy's capabilities, the better you can choose a game plan. At this point, the enemy obviously knows where you are, so you might as well turn your radar on and lock him up (if you haven't done so already). You can always deactivate the radar once the dogfight begins. Locking the target gives you detailed information about his energy status (altitude and airspeed).

The Su-27's twin turbofans provide a lot of thrust, making the vertical an attrac-

Never fight on the enemy's terms.

tive option against many older foes (like the MiG-23) or bandits moving significantly slower than you. An F-16 tends to keep the fight horizontal and at high G levels. Your Su-27 can't outturn an F-16, so you probably want to move into the vertical when fighting a Falcon. If the bandit has a lot of energy, like a fast-moving F-15 or Su-27, you should fight in the horizontal; there's no sense fighting on his terms if he has an advantage.

One Circle or Two?

Next, will you initiate a one-circle or a two-circle fight? A two-circle fight commences when both fighters pass each other and turn *toward* each other, as figure 4-10 shows. A one-circle fight begins when one fighter turns *away* from the other, as figure 4-11 shows. What's the difference?

A two-circle fight works best when you have a "turn-rate" advantage. Regardless of your turn radius, you crank the nose around the circle faster than the bandit and you wind up looking at his six. Figure 4-10 shows a fairly neutral situation where both aircraft turn at about the same rate. If, however, you extend the Su-27's turn circle another 90 degrees, you can see the angular advantage it gains over the F-15.

With a two-circle fight, you want to maximize the separation between you and the bandit at the merge. That separation forms the radius of your turn circle. You must complete as much of the turn as you can without crossing the bandit's flight path. In general, you want at least twice the distance of your turn radius between you and the bandit. Accordingly, the aircraft in figure 4-10 are way too close to effectively initiate a two-circle fight.

On the other hand, a one-circle fight works best when you have a "turn-radius" advantage. As exaggerated in figure 4-11, the Su-27's turn radius advantage lets it turn inside the F-15, then snake back onto its six. Actually, the Su-27 does not have such a significant advantage over the F-15, but the exaggerated figure illustrates the point.

With a one-circle fight, you try to minimize the separation between you and the bandit at the merge. Mentally move the Su-27 in figure 4-11 an inch to the right. Unless the illustrated Su-27 can *significantly* decrease its turn radius, it cannot complete the S turn without crossing outside the F-15's turn.

Note that one- and two-circle labels apply to *both* horizontal and vertical fights. Instead of minimizing or maximizing horizontal separation, you increase or decrease vertical separation for a two- or one-circle fight, respectively. Keep in mind, though, that gravity alters the shape of a vertical turn, stretching the turn circle into an egg shape.

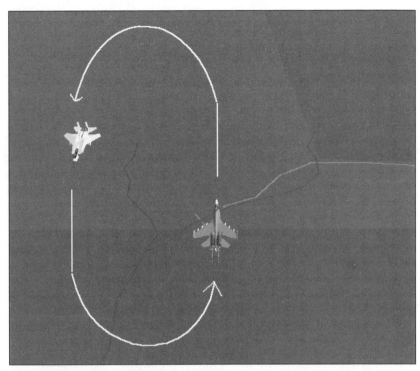

Figure 4-10 A Two-Circle Fight

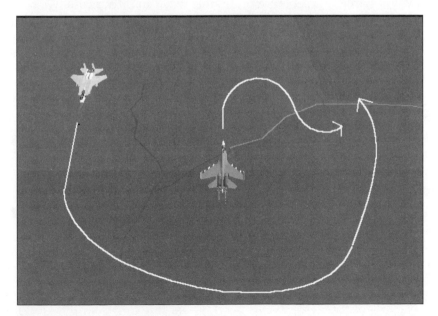

Figure 4-11 A One-Circle Fight

Examples

Suppose you're flying at 700 km/hr directly toward another Su-27 flying at 1200 km/hr for a left-to-left pass (that is, each aircraft passes down the left side of the other). For whatever reason, neither side fires a barrage of missiles. What do you do? First, increase throttle to full afterburner. Second, steer slightly to the right to increase lateral separation. Your next move depends on what the bandit does. If you both go high, his greater speed will cause him to overshoot. You'll have one good shot opportunity before your airspeed runs out. If you don't kill him quickly he'll swoop back down on you as your nose wallows at 300 km/hr. Alternatively, you could dive. This helps boost your speed and keeps a generally neutral situation until either he dives on you or you climb up into him.

If he keeps the fight horizontal, you probably shouldn't turn with him. He's got 500 km/hr more smash than you do, letting him maintain a hard, high-G turn longer than you. You don't have enough energy to go very high, so nose low, slice back may be your best initial option.

Now, suppose you're at 900 km/hr approaching an F-16 also at 900 km/hr for a right-to-right pass. The F-16 almost definitely will keep the fight horizontal. Generally, a single F-16 in *Su-27* will break into you, initiating a two-circle fight. If you face two F-16s, one usually turns into you while the other turns away, setting up a separate one-circle fight. In either case, your Su-27 is at a definite disadvantage in the horizontal plane. Most likely, you should light the afterburners and take your Su-27 high, then slice the nose back into the F-16s.

WVR Fight

At this point, you're committed to a within-visual-range (WVR) fight. Now its time to show your dogfighting skills. Ideally, you set up an initial advantage at the merge, and now you must use your aircraft's strengths to exploit that advantage. It's time for Basic Fighter Maneuvers (BFM).

BFM

Unfortunately, many simulation pilots equate BFM with high G-loads. They roll the wings, pull 9 G, and wait for the target to appear in the HUD. Such tactics will get an Su-27 pilot killed. Space constraints prevent a full discussion of BFM but I discuss a few common techniques in the following sections.

The Yo-Yo

The high yo-yo is arguably the most basic fighter maneuver. You use the high yo-yo to correct a high aspect angle, usually caused by closing too fast on a turning target. As figure 4-12 shows, the attacking Su-27 is closing too fast on the turning F-16. The Su-27 rolls out of the turn slightly and pulls up.

Figure 4-12 Commencing the High Yo-Yo

In figure 4-13 the Su-27 pulls back down into the turn. Notice how the Su-27's wings now align with the F-16's. Using one yo-yo, the Su-27 corrected a large aspect angle and situated itself directly behind the F-16.

Use the high yo-yo in a turning fight with any of the following circumstances:

1. You're about to over shoot the target.
2. You have too high an aspect angle for an effective shot, especially during gun attacks.
3. You can't match the target's turn.

Figure 4-13 The Result of the Yo-Yo

Figure 4-14 The Pitch Back   **Figure 4-15** The Slice Back

Pitch Back

The pitch back is a vertical maneuver similar to a half-loop, only banked during the climb. Instead of merely pulling straight up, the aircraft banks first, then pulls up. (See figure 4-14.) The pitch back is an effective turn after the merge, especially if the bandit stays relatively horizontal. It lets you convert some airspeed into altitude, thereby tightening your turn, without translating *all* your speed into altitude.

Slice Back

The slice back maneuver is similar to the split S, only the aircraft rolls less than 180 degrees before beginning the pull. The slice back provides a good first turn when merging with a faster bandit. The nose low attitude helps regain altitude, although gravity tends to elongate the turn.

The Lag Roll

An extension of the high yo-yo, the lag roll prevents an imminent overshoot and increases range to the target. As figure 4-16 shows, the attacker closes on a turning target, then pitches up as if to execute a yo-yo. The aircraft continues rolling, however, and completes a barrel roll around the defender's flight path. The conversion into the vertical points the attacker's lift vector away from the target, preventing an overshoot. Also, the conversion into the vertical bleeds speed, slowing the attacker. Reducing speed not only helps prevent overshooting, but also

Figure 4-16 The Lag Roll

increases range to the target. The lag roll is especially useful when you've closed beneath your missile's minimum launch distance and need to increase the range.

 ## The Furball

If you fly enough combat sorties, you'll eventually find yourself in a furball, or multiple-aircraft dogfight. Furballs differ significantly from one-on-one dogfights. There's always another bandit out there maneuvering onto your six. If you stop to chase one target, his wingman will come after you.

The paper "No Guts—No Glory" by Maj. Gen. Frederick C. Blesse laid a foundation of offensive and defensive tactical principles. For years this work was regarded the fighter pilot's bible. Blesse downed nine MiG-15s and one La-9 during the Korean War. Blesse outlined strategies for numerous furball situations—two being attacked by four, four being attacked by two, and so on. Many of these strategies are still valid for modern air combat.

One Attacking Many

If you find yourself in the unenviable position of single-handedly attacking a group of enemy aircraft, first identify the number of target aircraft. Patrols often fly in four-ship formations, sometimes spacing one two-ship element slightly behind the lead two-ship element. If you see only two aircraft in the target group, look around and verify there's not another two-ship tucked somewhere behind you. If there are two enemy aircraft, move in on the wingman first. *Never maneuver between the wingman and his wingleader!* If there are four aircraft, attack the trailing element first.

Assuming a guns-only attack, if possible attack from well above and behind the targets. Dive down toward the number four ship, keeping speed high. Strafe the formation starting with the number four aircraft and working toward the number one aircraft. Once the formation breaks (or an overshoot appears imminent), break outside the number four aircraft and convert your airspeed back into altitude.

If you're attacking the four-ship with missiles, try to stay above the formation while maneuvering into launch range. If you haven't been detected, close and engage with heat-seeking missiles. Using only the EOS, Shlem, or Fio HUD mode, lock onto the number four aircraft without using radar. After firing a missile, immediately target the number three aircraft, then the number two, and finally the leader. Try to have all four missiles in the air before the first one hits the trailing aircraft.

It's unlikely all missiles will kill all targets. The surviving bandits will most likely split. While one tries to occupy your attention, the other circles around behind you. When computer-controlled aircraft panic, they often enter a spiraling power dive. They blast right down to the deck, leveling off just a few hundred meters above the ground. Never follow a bandit down to the deck when there's an unengaged bandit hunting you. It wastes all your energy and leaves you a sitting duck for the unengaged bandit. Diving for the deck takes the bandit out of the fight for a few moments, giving you time to assess your next move.

Once you've broken the formation, you have two choices—run or stay. If you run, point the nose toward friendly territory, light the afterburners, and dive for the deck. Keep your speed at maximum until you're safely inside friendly territory. If you decide to stay, generally convert your speed back into altitude and hunt the highest surviving bandit. Don't drag the bandits down to the deck unless you *know* you have superior thrust. If you're fighting slow, heavy adversaries like MiG-23s, you might opt to dive for the deck, drag them down into the weeds, then light the afterburners and climb above them.

Two Attacking Many

If you have a wingman with you, your tactics are basically the same; however use your wingman to increase your firepower. During the initial attack, select the trailing target and order your wingman to attack it. Quickly select the number three ship and fire a missile at it yourself. Now, target the number two ship and order the wingman to engage while you attack the leader.

When the formation breaks, order the wingman to attack whatever target you currently have locked. While he presses the attack, you should break high and search for survivors who may be circling back on either you or the wingman. If the wingman is in no immediate threat, you're free to engage other targets. If the wingman is in danger, engage the bandit threatening him. If there's only one survivor, leave the wingman to engage, extend away and climb, then come back into the fight. The bandit will be too busy maneuvering away from your wingman to evade your medium-range missile shots.

Alternatively, when attacking four bandits you might try a bait-and-switch approach. Dive onto the second element, opening fire as necessary. Once the trailing bandits believe you're attacking them, they'll break into some defensive posture, probably a full-power, spiraling dive that effectively removes them from the fight for several seconds. Now, immediately retarget the lead element and fire before they can obtain a neutral position.

When attacking a formation of four experienced, computer-controlled pilots the bandits will usually break away at four- to five-second intervals while the leader continues straight and level. While you focus on the main group, the wingmen circle behind you. It's imperative, therefore, that you attack the number four aircraft first and work your way up the formation to the leader.

One Attacked By Many

If you're alone and attacked by three or four bandits, you have a real problem. Airspeed can be your salvation. You need enough energy to turn into each bandit as it attacks you. Above all else, *do not panic*. Keep calm and conserve your energy, executing a max performance turn whenever a bandit initiates an attack. Unfortunately, the Su-27's poor rear visibility makes this a difficult task. The bandits usually break off into singles and press the attack one at a time. Try to monitor their positions and watch for gaps between them. Work on pointing your nose toward friendly territory, then execute a full-after-burner dive toward home through a gap in their formation.

Don't necessarily try to be offensive. *Never try to track a single target!* Switch off your radar, activate EOS and Shlem, and shoot anything that crosses your nose. Never reverse your turn during this kind of a furball, no matter how juicy the target.

Two Attacked By Many

As with one-attacked-by-many, the two must keep a strong defensive turn going. It's still unwise to reverse your turn; however, you should make a reasonable effort to defend your wingman. On the average, order him to cover your six immediately after the attack. Once you locate a specific target, dispatch him to attack it while you press against a different target.

Conclusion

The furball is a difficult, confusing situation complicated by *Su-27*'s few wingman commands and absent radio communications. Your situational awareness must stay high—keep track of *everybody*. If you lose track of a bandit you can generally expect him to reappear directly on your tail.

CHAPTER FIVE

Mission Planning and Campaign Strategies

When you take command of Squadron or General missions (or create your own missions from scratch), you assume responsibility for more than just you and your wingman. Now, all assets in-theater follow your orders. If they succeed, the glory is yours. If they fail, the blame falls squarely on *your* shoulders. How do you ensure victory under these conditions? By using the same basic principals associated with individual achievement: Know the strengths and weaknesses of your forces, know the strengths and weaknesses of the enemy forces, then develop a plan to exploit your strengths against their weaknesses.

Analysis of Available Aircraft

Su-27 includes 13 different aircraft types, including the Flanker. Each has different strengths, weaknesses, and missions; some aren't even fighters. If you understand the role each aircraft plays on the battlefield, you not only can employ your own assets more effectively, you can evaluate more accurately the risk posed by enemy forces. AWACS just detected a flight of four enemy F-16s heading toward a friendly base; do they pose a significant threat or substantially impede accomplishing your mission goals?

The answer, of course, depends on many things. First, what's going on at the friendly base in question? Are any aircraft preparing to launch or recover there? Are these aircraft capable of defending themselves against F-16s? Have these aircraft completed their mission yet? What weapons do the F-16s carry? Do the F-16s pose a threat to the base?

On the real battlefield, these questions often evoke complex and conditional answers based on the quality and quantity of intelligence available to mission planners. The F-16 is generally regarded as the world's best close-range dogfighter, but it was used exclusively as air-to-ground attack aircraft during the Gulf War. In the real world, we have little means to determine what threat the F-16s pose without actually seeing the aircraft and observing their armament. (Of course, today's electronic battlefield offers many ways of "seeing" the enemy.)

In the simulated world, however, some of these questions have fixed answers. The personal computer can't possibly create all the dynamics of the modern battlefield in anything remotely resembling real time. If the computer tried to mimic every aspect of the war, the simulation would run at a fraction of a snail's pace. Game designers are aware of this, and make some concessions that reduce the number of possible answers to the foregoing questions. In *Su-27* most of these concessions deal with the types of weapons the aircraft can carry. This section assesses the capabilities of the 12 other aircraft, examines these concessions, and describes how they impede or support your mission.

A-50

The A-50 is the airborne eyes of the military. These powerful AWACS provide the Su-27, MiG-29, and other aircraft with a view of the entire airborne battlefield. Although the tail gunner will open fire at close range, these giants are virtually defenseless in the simulated world. They depend entirely on ground-based surface-to-air defenses and friendly fighters for their survival.

Typically, you want to position the A-50 well behind the aerial front lines at an altitude of 10,000 m. Keep at least one flight on CAP between the front and the A-50 along the anticipated threat axis. MiG-29s and Su-27s equipped with R-77s and R-73s make the best AWACS defenders, but any fighter available is better than no fighter protection at all! If convenient, try to intercept enemy A-50s but don't expend considerable resources doing so. Removing

Figure 5-1 The A-50

the A-50 blinds enemy fighters but doesn't stop his attack aircraft from proceeding toward their targets. The enemy probably stationed numerous airborne and ground-based defenses near the A-50, making it a very dangerous target to attack.

F-15

For decades, the F-15 has been hailed as the greatest air superiority aircraft in the world. Designed to counter the MiG-25 (when Western analysts believed the MiG-25 to be an insurmountable superfoe), the F-15 was built to impressive standards. The first fighter with a thrust-to-weight ratio exceeding 1.0 at combat weight, the F-15 combines flight performance, impressive avionics, and a relatively large missile payload. Although not the most nimble dogfighter, the F-15 can hold its own and often maneuvers in the vertical.

Su-27 offers only one missile package for the F-15, a mixture of four AIM-120 AMRAAMs and four AIM-9 Sidewinders, the former being an incredibly accurate and deadly radar-guided missile and the latter a battle-proven heat-seeker. Used only for air-to-air combat (the F-15E variant is not simulated), the F-15 works well on either CAP or Intercept missions. F-15s make excellent AWACS guardians. If enemy F-15s vector toward friendly bombers

Figure 5-2 The F-15

or ground-attack aircraft, immediately maneuver to intercept. The F-15 provides no threat to ground targets. If hostile F-15s approach a friendly base they're either attempting to attack your forces during takeoffs and landings, or they're clearing an airborne corridor for enemy strike aircraft. If the base is well defended with SAMs and AAA, assume the air defenses can handle their own and focus your attention *behind* the F-15s. Although dogfighting may be fun, attempt to destroy the strike aircraft without engaging the F-15s. It doesn't matter how many fighters you shoot down if the enemy destroys your home airfield.

F-16

U.S. military planners quickly realized the venerable F-15 was as costly as it was capable. A superfighter by any definition, the U.S. Air Force simply couldn't afford enough of them to fill its combat commitments. The USAF decided to supplement the relatively small F-15 fleet with a large fleet of "less capable" aircraft. The F-16 seemed the perfect choice.

The F-16 is the best close-range dogfighter in the world. There's no better fighter to take into a "knife fight in a phonebooth" than the F-16. Officially called the "Fighting Falcon," its pilots usually call it the "Viper." It

Figure 5-3 The F-16

doesn't have the impressive avionics of the F-15, but it carries a formidable mix of air-to-air and air-to-ground weapons. Designers limited simulated F-16, however, to a mix of AIM-120 and AIM-9 missiles. In *Su-27*, F-16s can't carry any air-to-ground weapons. Subsequently, in *Su-27* you should assign the F-16 the same roles as the F-15—protecting AWACS and clearing a path for ingressing strike aircraft.

You can't specify an escort, intercept, or fighter sweep mission for the F-16. You must use a combination of CAP waypoints to accomplish any of these tasks. An inbound F-16 represents little threat to ground targets, but it poses a substantial threat to other aircraft, especially slow, defenseless attack aircraft. The AIM-120 gives the F-16 a fairly long-range punch, so don't let one anywhere near your AWACS aircraft.

IL-76

The IL-76 replaced the An-12 "Cub" as the Soviet's primary civil and military transport. The IL-76 can carry supplies, insert paratroopers, and extract wounded while operating from short, rough runways in bad weather. In the real world, the IL-76's troop transporting capability makes this lumbering

Figure 5-4 The IL-76

behemoth a respectable threat. The simulated IL-76, however, lacks any meaningful combat capability. Although you may encounter tail gun fire at close ranges, the simulated IL-76 is, for all practical purposes, little more than a commercial airliner in a combat zone. You'll rarely need to deploy them yourself; nor will you need to intercept enemy IL-76s.

MiG-23

The MiG-23 succeeded the MiG-21. A substantially improved radar (probably based on radar equipment gathered from crashed F-4s in Vietnam), bigger payload, faster speed, and longer range made the MiG-23 one of the Soviet Union's most important fighters. The variable-geometry, or swing wing, design improves maneuverability and takeoff and landing performance. Unfortunately, the MiG-23 never compared favorably to any of its Western contemporaries.

The MiG-23 is a mediocre fighter, so avoid deploying it when better fighters are available. It carries only the relatively short-range R-23 and R-60 air-to-air missiles. The R-23R has a maximum range of 35 km, but is SARH and requires the launcher to maintain radar lock until the missile strikes its target. As explained in Chapter 4, this leaves the launcher vulnerable to

Figure 5-5 The MiG-23

counterattack. The heat-seeking R-60, meanwhile, has a maximum range of only 10 km and lacks significant killing power. The MiG-23 can carry a mediocre air-to-ground load of a few iron bombs and rockets, but is generally insufficient for the task.

You'll best use the MiG-23 as a second-line defense. Send the more capable aircraft to the front and into enemy territory while holding MiG-23s in reserve behind the lines to engage stray attack aircraft and bombers. It would take a very large MiG-23 fleet to stop a substantial enemy air raid, although it can effectively engage strike aircraft while more modern platforms (like the Su-27) engage any escorting fighters. If the enemy sends MiG-23s into friendly territory, let the SAMs and AAA handle them. If your bases are well defended, the MiG-23 poses little threat.

MiG-27

Introduced in the latter half of the 1970s, the MiG-27 derives from the MiG-23 designed specifically for the air-to-ground role. Retaining the basic airframe, the MiG-27 focuses on slow-speed, low-altitude flight. Its weapon's payload was increased over the MiG-23, and the aircraft poses a substan-

Figure 5-6 The MiG-27

tially greater threat to ground units. The MiG-27 carries a wide assortment of air-to-ground weapons, including anti-radiation missiles, precision guided missiles, and anti-ship missiles. Still suffering from the MiG-23's mediocre flight performance, the MiG-27 carries a much greater and deadlier ground attack capability.

The MiG-27, along with the Su-25 and Su-27, provides a major part of your offensive punch. It may not carry many weapons but its payload compares with other available strike aircraft. The MiG-27 can't survive a dogfight, but it presents a major threat to mobile ground units, radar sites, ships, and airfields. Use the MiG-27 to engage enemy units with ground-attack missiles from long range, especially to destroy enemy radar sites before another strike group arrives. You can't ignore the threat enemy MiG-27s present, and should intercept them as soon as possible.

MiG-29

Western observers often conclude, inaccurately, that the Su-27 and MiG-29 were really a single design program that copied U.S. aircraft. The twin fins, the blended body, and other aspects support this view. But the MiG-29 did not

Figure 5-7 The MiG-29

copy the Su-27, nor was the Su-27 "stolen" from the MiG-29. Although the two aircraft are very similar in appearance (many Western observers can't distinguish between them despite the difference in size), they resulted from two distinct design programs using common research data. Both teams reportedly drew the same conclusions from that data, and designed two similar aircraft. Reportedly, designers at Sukhoi and Mikoyan-Gurevich bristle at the suggestion that they stole each other's ideas or copied Western aircraft designs.

The MiG-29 reportedly uses the same avionics suite as the Su-27. The MiG has the same radar, the same EOS, the same Shlem helmet system, and the same air-to-air weapons. This means it can attack without revealing itself and can take high-aspect missile shots across the circle. Because it is smaller and lighter, the MiG-29 is probably a better dogfighter in terms of maneuverability. The MiG-29, however, can't carry as much payload as the Su-27. In an air-to-air configuration, it can't carry as many air-to-air missiles as your Flanker. In an air-to-ground configuration, it can't carry as much weight or as many weapon types. It can't carry any air-to-ground missiles, and can carry only a variety of iron bombs.

For the most part you should use (and expect the enemy to use) the MiG-29 as an air-to-air platform. It's a respectable ground-attack platform, but other aircraft can do that job significantly better. You should intercept MiG-29 anytime one vectors toward a less-maneuverable, defenseless aircraft such as a bomber or dedicated ground-attack aircraft. The MiG-29 could be carrying long-range air-to-air missiles, so expedite the intercept. The MiG-29 can't attack ground targets without approaching extremely close (in modern combat terms) and dropping iron bombs. The MiG-29 poses little threat to targets heavily defended by SAMs and AAA, therefore, but it may wreak havoc on lightly defended targets or unarmed convoys.

Su-24

The first true variable-geometry aircraft to enter Soviet operation, the Su-24 is a reasonably impressive interdiction aircraft used primarily on defense suppression and hard-target raids. Its highly accurate navigational system and terrain-following radar systems make it an ideal low-level penetrator. Although not very effective against mobile targets such as tanks and APVs, it's an outstanding weapon against ships and fixed targets like runways and bridges.

The Su-24 can be used in defense suppression strikes ahead of the main package, low-level penetration missions deep into enemy territory, or massed

Figure 5-8 The Su-24

attacks on fixed targets. It carries roughly three times the payload of a MiG-27 (in addition to significantly more advanced avionics). Consider the Su-24 a high-priority threat and move to intercept as soon as possible. Always remember that the Su-24 carries long-range missiles and engages ground targets from standoff distance. You can't ignore the Su-24.

Su-25

The Su-25 is perhaps the deadliest attack aircraft in *Su-27*'s arsenal. Designed to answer to the U.S.'s A-10, the Su-25 carries a payload a little less than half the Su-24's. The Su-25 encases the pilot in a titanium bathtub canopied with armored glass. Its wide variety of armaments lets it fly all manner of missions from anti-radar to anti-ship to runway denial to tank killing. The Su-25 is designed to operate near the front lines from rough, unimproved airstrips. It can also carry a kit containing tools, spare parts, auxiliary power supply, pump for manual refueling, and other "self-deployment" supplies, letting it operate from rough fields lacking support facilities.

Generally, use Su-24s with their larger payload to attack large, fixed tar-

Figure 5-9 The Su-25

gets while using Su-25s against smaller, more maneuverable targets. Its armor makes the Su-25 an effective tank hunter and AAA killer. Although somewhat vulnerable to SAMs, the Su-25 is designed to search the battlefield, hunting down targets and killing them. Su-25s can wreak havoc on any clustered target such as a convoy, a tank platoon, or an airbase. Ingressing at low level, the Su-25 pops up, destroys a building or vehicle, then ducks low behind the terrain and repositions for another attack.

Tu-22

An aging relic from the 1960s, the Tu-22 is a supersonic bomber designed primarily for maritime reconnaissance and strike missions. Supersonic speed makes it somewhat difficult to catch and a reasonably large payload gives it quite a punch. Long-range missiles let it attack from standoff range and keep it a viable platform 40 years after it was designed.

Besides the typical missile attacks against fixed targets and ships, the Tu-22 is an effective carpet bomber capable of delivering 30 FAB-500s on target. A group of four Tu-22s can drop 120 FAB-500s, producing results not unlike

Figure 5-10 The Tu-22

a massive artillery barrage. Provided the enemy lacks high-altitude SAMs, the Tu-22 should generally attack from high altitude. The Tu-22 has only one defense against enemy fighters—speed. If it can't outrun the bandit, it's dead. Given this shortcoming, the Tu-22 should be heavily escorted both to and from the target area.

Tu-95

In service for over 40 years, the Tu-95 "Bear" has become the backbone, if not the very symbol, of Soviet (and now Russian) strategic bombing capability. For decades, U.S. fighters have flown practice intercepts against Bear bombers practicing attack runs on the U.S. NATO aircraft around the world, from Alaska to Europe, have performed similar practice runs for decades; each side tries to measure the other's response capabilities.

The Tu-95 carries about the same payload as the Tu-22, but at a much slower speed. The Tu-95 makes can carpet bomb by carrying 26 FAB-500 bombs; attack fixed ground targets from long range with Kh-15 or Kh-55 missiles, or attack ships with Kh-15s. It's subsonic, so the Tu-95 is fairly easy to

Figure 5-11 The Tu-95

catch and should be escorted at all times. When possible, the escort should move ahead of the Tu-95 in a fighter sweep.

Tu-142

The Tu-142, a specialized version of the Tu-95, entered service in the early 1970s. The Tu-142 focuses on the maritime attack role, carries a variety of anti-ship missiles, and boasts avionics and fuselage improvements.

Figure 5-12 The Tu-142

Attack Profiles

How aircraft attack a particular target varies with the nature of the target, surface-to-air defenses near the target, the weapons available, and the aircraft delivering the weapons.

High Altitude

High altitude, above 8,000 m, offers sanctuary from low-altitude air defenses such as AAA and complicates intercepts by older fighters such as the MiG-23. The aircraft can usually engage the target from farther away while conserving fuel by flying more efficiently. High altitude increases the range of ground radars in the Su-27 (and other aircraft), letting the pilot pick up and acquire targets from farther away. This gives the pilot more time to tune the targeting cross hairs and line up for the attack. Unfortunately, aircraft at high altitude are easier to detect and quite vulnerable to long-range SAMs. In general, high-altitude attacks are not advisable unless long range SAMs, such as the S-300, have been neutralized first.

Figure 5-13 During high-altitude attacks, the CCIP indicator is not visible without diving.

High-altitude attacks offer a serious disadvantage for tactical attack aircraft dropping iron bombs. In most high-altitude attacks, the CCIP indicator lies so far beneath the aircraft that it's not visible in the HUD. The aircraft has to dive steeply so the pilot can see the CCIP indicator. The aircraft picks up substantial speed during the dive, eating away altitude and bringing the aircraft closer and closer to AAA range. The pilot is forced to make quick targeting decisions and maneuvers, then pull out of the dive as soon as possible. In the real world, some aircraft can't release ordnance at the speeds reached during such a dive; however, this is not a factor in *Su-27*.

During the early days of the 1991 Gulf War, many coalition aircraft flew low-altitude attacks to avoid radar detection. After the Iraqi defense network was crushed, however, the danger from high-altitude SAMs was minimal while AAA and small-arms fire remained respectable threats. Accordingly, once the SAM threat was neutralized, most Coalition aircraft flew higher attack profiles to avoid gunfire.

Medium Altitude

Medium-altitude attacks offer a variety of advantages mixed with serious disadvantages. Staying at 1,000 to 8,000 m, generally keeps the flight above

Figure 5-14 A Medium Altitude Attack

AAA, small arms, and shoulder-launched missiles, but puts the flight right in the middle of most SAMs' engagement envelopes. Pilots flew many sorties at medium altitude during the Gulf War, but didn't fly this profile until the SAM threat was sufficiently minimized.

The medium-altitude attack provides the same benefits as the high-altitude attack, albeit on a reduced scale. It lets pilots locate targets at longer range than low-altitude attacks, and avoid low-altitude air defenses. The primary advantage of the medium-altitude profile is the location of the CCIP indicator on the HUD. Although the aircraft usually still needs to dive, the dive need not be nearly as steep as with high-altitude attacks.

Low Altitude

If the enemy's air defense network is still operational, low-altitude (below 1,000 m) is the attack profile of choice. Very-low-altitude flying (below 100 m), called *nape of the earth* (NOE) flying, skims just above the treetops using hills and other obstructions to hide behind. Many modern attack aircraft designed for NOE flight carry terrain-following *radar* (TFR) that maps the landscape ahead of the aircraft. The TFR communicates the terrain to the autopilot, which automatically maneuvers the aircraft to maintain a constant altitude (say, 75 m).

Flying so low puts the aircraft at greater risk from small arms, but usually puts the aircraft *well below* most SAMs' engagement zones. Since radar can't penetrate hills and other obstacles, flying so low greatly reduces risk of detection. Usually, the reduced detection risk far outweighs any danger from small arms. Low-altitude flight, especially at high speed, carries a greater risk of crashing than the other attack profiles. Many strike pilots have died when their aircraft rammed into the ground at high speed, especially when late-night darkness makes flying at low altitude even more hazardous.

Not all weapons are usable at low altitude. Some missiles fall a few meters before the motor engages and propels them toward the target. Iron bombs have a fairly large blast radius. Since the bombs don't fall as far, they explode sooner, often trapping the launching aircraft in their *blast radius*. Its own weapons' explosions can seriously damage attacking aircraft. Some aircraft carry bombs equipped with small parachutes that slow their fall and let the aircraft escape, but the Su-27 carries no such system.

This leaves you with only two alternatives: First, the Su-27 can execute a "pop-up" attack. The jet approaches the target zone from very low altitude, using the terrain to mask its presence. Just as it reaches the target area, the pilot pitches up sharply, rolls the jet inverted, locates the target, rolls the jet back to the target, drops the bombs, and dives for the deck. This gives the pilot an opportunity to survey the target zone and select the best target, while the increased altitude puts the aircraft safely outside its weapons' blast radius. On the downside, the pop-up maneuver exposes the aircraft to every anti-aircraft gun, every SAM missile, and every Bedouin with an AK-47.

Second, the Su-27 can increase speed as much as possible. The aircraft comes screaming in at maximum speed, releases the bombs, and escapes before they explode. This method keeps the aircraft near the ground and away from enemy fire, but the increased speed complicates the attack. Flying faster at lower altitude means there's less time to recover from mistakes. Any minor error often results in a fatal crash under these circumstances. The increased speed also reduces targeting time, meaning the pilot must locate, identify, target, and attack the objective in much less time.

Missiles versus Bombs

Attack profiles vary depending on the type of ordnance involved. Although the normal ingress altitude restrictions still apply, the direction from which the aircraft attacks changes based on weapon and target types. You don't attack a convoy of moving vehicles from the same direction using missiles as you do using iron bombs.

Beam Attacks

Beam basically means a 90-degree aspect angle. For example, an aircraft off your right wing is *abeam* of you. If you approach a target from a 90-degree aspect angle, you're abeam of the target. In terms of ground targets, imagine a long, single-file convoy of vehicles moving down a road. Approaching the convoy from the side executes a beam approach. Approaching from the beam offers this primary advantage: When attacking with air-to-ground missiles you can see the entire width of the convoy and pick out the most valuable targets. Beam attacks work well when using missiles but not using iron bombs (see following "Line Attacks" section).

Further, beam attacks let you deliver ordnance, then break away without overflying the targets. The closer you get to the target, the greater the risk from AAA and other ground fire.

Line Attacks

Imagine that convoy again. This time, fly directly over the road toward its end. You're now attacking the line. Line attacks offer one major advantage: You line up once with the lead target, then sequentially deliver (or *ripple*) iron bombs as you fly over the targets. If you align exactly with the target's longitudinal axis, you need only aim once to deliver multiple weapons. Targets don't need to be perfectly aligned single file, although it helps. If the targets are roughly aligned along the same axis you can fly a slight zigzag pattern, weaving from target to target with minimal flight path changes.

Line attacks have one major problem: You fly directly over the target. Sometimes there's no alternative, but doing so increases the risk from ground fire.

Combinations

Aircraft such as the Su-25 and A-10 often make a series of combination attacks. The Su-27 can, also, but remember: The more times you fly over the target the more chances they have to shoot you down. Often, attacking aircraft approach the convoy's line from either end and destroy the lead and trailing vehicles, trapping the remainder between the burning hulks. The attackers then execute a series of pop-up attacks from various beam approaches, slowly and methodically picking off each survivor.

Combination attacks work best when multiple aircraft attack at seemingly random intervals. In *Su-27*, try ordering two separate flights to attack the same area from low altitude. One aircraft can attack while the other repositions, preoccupying enemy air defenses and confusing enemy forces.

Multiple Strikes

A single flight of attack aircraft may be sufficient to remove a bridge. It takes considerably more firepower, however, to shut down an airfield. An air base has one or more runways which must be destroyed; control towers and other buildings which must be taken down; early warning radars to detect your approach; heavy SAM and AAA defenses, as well as fighters capable of intercepting your group.

Therefore, you probably need fighters to sweep the area ahead of the strike package; defense suppression aircraft to eliminate targeting radars; escort fighters to pick up any remaining enemy fighters; close air support

(CAS) aircraft to take out AAA threats; bombers for the primary buildings, and attack aircraft for each runway. Of course, you rarely have enough aircraft to fulfill all these roles, forcing you to make hard decisions about where to use your limited assets. Even after you decide which assets to use, you must still determine route, timing, and weapons packages. These are tough decisions, but that's the role of a theater or squadron commander.

Timing

Timing is the most critical aspect of any attack. If the fighter sweep arrives at the target too soon, enemy SAMs pick them apart. If the anti-radar sweep attacks before the fighter sweep gets there, enemy defensive CAP knock them from the sky. If the fighter sweep departs too early, the enemy may field more fighters to intercept the main strike package. If the anti-radar aircraft arrive too late, the SAMs and AAA decimate the main strike. In the real world, aircraft receive specific time-on-target orders and are expected to arrive at the specified target within no more than 20 to 30 seconds from the specified time. Lives are on the line and any delay, even 10 seconds, could allow an enemy missile launch.

Su-27, unfortunately, doesn't allow this level of precision. You can specify waypoint arrival times, but these are approximate numbers. The manual explains that the aircraft try to arrive at waypoints reasonably close to the specified time but makes no guarantees. You can still coordinate your attacks, but not with the precision of real-world military operations.

How should you time and coordinate your attacks? Generally speaking, fighters should launch first and assume a defensive position over your airfield. If you have enough aircraft available, leave these fighters to patrol near the home field for the entire mission. If you're short on available aircraft, give them enough waypoints around the field to keep them in the vicinity while the rest of the package launches, then add more waypoints and mission objectives as necessary.

About three to five minutes after the initial fighters launch, launch your AWACS. For most missions, you only need one. Remember, the AWACS is vulnerable to enemy counterattack and must be protected at all times. Within one minute of launching the AWACS, launch additional fighters programed to escort and protect it. They should stay with the AWACS until it reaches its assigned patrol zone, then should maneuver about 50 km away placing themselves between the AWACS and the anticipated threat zone.

About five minutes later the fighter sweep and anti-radar aircraft should launch. If you're attacking ships, an enemy base, or any heavily defended target, *always* send a group of anti-radar aircraft ahead of the main strike package. The anti-radar aircraft and the fighter sweep aircraft should reach the target zone within 30 seconds of each other. Keep in mind, however, that anti-radar aircraft can engage from relatively long distances; that is, it can fly safely behind the fighter cover and still engage enemy radar sites on schedule.

Launch the main strike about three to five minutes after the anti-radar aircraft. Launch aircraft in pairs, assigning each pair a different mission—one pair "pinpoint strike," the next "CAS," and so on. They should launch as quickly as possible and arrive at the target less than two minutes after the anti-radar and fighter sweep aircraft. This means the strike aircraft must fly fast enough to make up one to two minutes during ingress. Always launch these aircraft in pairs. Only two aircraft can take off at a time. If you specify more than two in a given group, the first two take off, then the second two, then they waste time joining up en route to the target. If you need four aircraft, launch them as independent pairs.

Target Selection and Resource Allocation

The obvious question, of course, is, "How do you know if you need two or four aircraft against a given target?" Some targets, like S-300 SAM launchers, can shoot down inbound missiles. Other targets, like runways, are fairly easy to find but difficult to shut down. How do you decide?

The decisions are never easy. You must make a judgment call, specify a plan, and proceed. A few guidelines, though, will help you through the process. First, consider enemy air defenses. SAM launchers, especially the S-300, are reasonably effective against inbound missiles. Most S-300 sites have a search radar, a tracking radar, and three or more missile launchers. If you launch one anti-radiation missile at an S-300 launcher you can rest assured the enemy will shoot it down. The S-300 can track and engage multiple targets at once. To destroy it you must overwhelm its capabilities. That may mean launching 10 missiles just to ensure one hits the target. The ratio of launched missiles to those that actually survive enemy defenses is called *cost of entry*. In other words, how many missiles does it cost to score a single hit?

Given the limited weapons packages available in *Su-27*, strike aircraft can't carry more than two or three anti-radiation missiles. At best, an Su-25 can carry two Kh-31p and one Kh-25 missiles. An Su-27 can carry up to four

Kh-31p and two Kh-29 missiles. A flight of four Su-27s could field 16 long-range anti-radiation missiles and conduct a follow-up attack with Kh-29s after the radars are down. Unfortunately, the computer-controlled aircraft tend to launch missiles one at a time. When engaging missile sites, especially S-300s, try sending a series of single-aircraft flights to the same target at the same time. Although they still tend to fire one missile at a time, they seem to engage concurrently, increasing the number of simultaneously inbound missiles.

For runways, a single pair of KMGU-2–equipped aircraft are sufficient for a single runway. If dropped with *extreme* accuracy exactly in the middle of a runway, 30 KMGU-2s will render a runway useless. However, the computer-controlled aircraft usually don't attack with such accuracy. Assigning each flight a single runway guarantees closure of that runway. If the target airfield has more than one runway, use a separate flight to attack the other strip. Remember, runways are longer than normal operations require. If you damage only one end, aircraft can still take off and land on the undisturbed portion. You must, therefore, crater the center of the runway, leaving no undisturbed length greater than 600 m (approximately three runway hash marks).

When attacking the rest of the air base, allow two aircraft for every four to six target buildings. Armed with Kh-29s, a single aircraft can effectively engage two to four buildings (depending on the aircraft's payload).

The simulated anti-ship missiles carry quite a punch. Usually only one is required to down even the largest ship. Most warships, however, have anti-missile defenses sufficient to down a barrage of inbound missiles. As with SAM launchers, you must allow for a high cost of entry. Sending an anti-radiation to knock out the ship's radar before the strike package arrives substantially reduces cost of entry. Most available strike aircraft carry only two anti-ship missiles. When attacking a large group of warships, deploy a generous number of anti-radiation aircraft followed by an equally generous number of anti-ship aircraft.

When attacking vehicles, bridges, fuel tanks, or other small objects, primarily use the Kh-29, when possible. This precision missile is highly effective against all target types (except some large buildings). Generally, if you're attacking a bridge or railroad, only one aircraft is necessary against the target itself. The nature of the air defense network, however, may require an anti-radiation strike ahead of the main package. Generally, use the Su-25 against armored convoys; its armor and durability permit more passes over the target with less risk to the pilot.

Escort: Close, Wide, Forward, Reception

Most of the time, bombers and attack aircraft should have fighter escorts. Many players visualize escort duties based on old World War II movies: The fighters fly in close formation with the bombers, then break off and attack the bandits. In the modern, long-range battlefield, the escort role takes on several new duties.

The fighter is most effective as a hunter–killer roaming the skies and sneaking up on unsuspecting prey. As an escort, however, the fighter is tied to the escort aircraft. It flies a relatively predictable path with a virtual bull's-eye painted on its side. The fighter should be free to maneuver, attack, and escape. It's not suited to creating an impenetrable barrier between hostile forces and defenders. Despite the best efforts of friendly pilots, a few bandits always seem to get through the escort, especially if they're equipped with long-range missiles.

Therefore, a layered defense tends to work better. Rings of aircraft assigned different tasks circle the main body and provide multiple layers of defense. Enemy fighters that break through one layer are intercepted by the next layer.

Forward escorts perform the standard fighter sweep mission. Consisting of two to four aircraft (depending on the threat's anticipated nature), they patrol from 100 to as much as 200 km ahead of the main formation. These attack all enemy aircraft while transmitting warnings to the main body. The forward escorts attempt to destroy the bandits, or at least drag the fight away from the main body.

Close escort is the basic, garden-variety escort mission. The fighters fly reasonably close to the escorted aircraft and engage any bandits that come too close. In *Su-27*, the "escort" mission provides this functionality. The escorting aircraft stick with the escorted aircraft all the way to the target and back. Ideally, separate close escorts flank each side of the main formation. Each flight spaces itself away from the main body about the same distance as the enemy's air-to-air weapons. No matter which side the formation is attacked from, a close-escort flight is available to engage. Most of the time, however, you have insufficient aircraft for such a thorough shield. In this case, you may position a single flight of close escorts between the main body and the hostiles along the anticipated threat axis. Close escort is probably the most frustrating mission a fighter pilot performs.

Long-range missiles, however, often let bandits engage the bombers well before the close escorts can maneuver to intercept. *Wide escorts*, therefore, patrol along the same axis as the close escorts, but much farther from the formation. Generally at least 50 to 100 km from the escort group, the wide escorts pick up and engage bandits before they get close. They attrit the inbound force, leaving any stragglers that manage to break through to the close escort.

Finally, the *reception escorts*, stationed at fixed points along the path of the main body's return route, provide reinforcements on the way home. As the returning group passes by, the reception escorts engage any trailing bandits. By this time, most forward, wide, and close escorts are low on fuel and ammunition, anyway. If enough aircraft are available, position a series of reception escorts along the return route. After the main formation returns to base, the reception escort farthest out breaks for home. After it passes a few reception checkpoints, the next-farthest group heads for home, and so on. The reception escort chain slowly collapses as the outermost aircraft continually return to base.

Escort pilots must rely heavily on their personal judgment. Because you have a strictly defensive role, attacking every bandit you detect isn't feasible. You must save your limited fuel and weapons to attack only those bandits posing a distinct threat to the main formation. Attacking a MiG-29 patrol 250 km from the formation may be fun and may improve your kill count, but it does nothing to ensure success of the overall mission. You may return to the formation low on fuel and weapons to find that a pair of lowly MiG-23s decimated the strike force. No amount of air-to-air kills will generate success if the main formation is destroyed before it reaches the target. Your goal as an escort pilot is to protect the main formation.

Fully implementing a layered escort requires a large number of aircraft. If only two aircraft are assigned to each mission, that's eight fewer aircraft available for other missions. If the mission requires SAM suppression and AWACS protection, the number of aircraft needed increases drastically. The cost of completely protecting the strike formation becomes prohibitively high.

Example Missions

When you must make difficult resource allocation decisions, consider the following guidelines:

1. *Always* use two aircraft per flight. In most cases, except for the aforementioned anti-radiation strikes, one aircraft is simply too vulnerable to enemy ambush. Large groups of wingmen, however, follow the leader's

motions. A group of four aircraft really only has one "thinker" and three followers. Dividing into two groups of two provides twice as many thinkers and only two followers.

2. Always have at least one flight flying air cover. Enemy fighters will always be out there looking for you and your allies. If you're flying the air cover mission, position a reception escort near your primary base. When you bug out low on ammunition and fuel it's nice to have somebody waiting to knock that last bandit off your trail. Nothing is more embarrassing than a lone bandit shooting you down while you're trying to land.

3. Long flights need more fuel. Each extra fuel tank the aircraft carries means one less hardpoint available for weapons. If the mission requires a long flight (and extra fuel), the aircraft may not be able to carry enough weapons to complete it. In this situation you may find yourself sending a dozen aircraft with one missile each to attack some distant target. In general, try to launch from the nearest friendly base and reduce flight time.

4. Use ECM pods even when you must sacrifice other weapons to do so. ECM is designed to save pilot lives. It's better to partially damage a target and bring all your pilots home than to lose four or five aircraft on a single attack.

Target Considerations

Your orders usually specify the exact mixture of aircraft available for each mission. In general, assume this to be the *minimum* number of aircraft required to complete the mission. In most cases, adding a few aircraft improves mission results.

Next, consider the target. How strong is it? How big is it? How many weapons do you need to destroy it? How many aircraft are required to carry that much ordnance? You'll probably never have the number of aircraft you need to fully complete the mission, so you must make some sacrifices.

Are there any enemy airfields near the target? GAI fighters may be holding position, waiting for you there. In this case, you probably need another group of fighters to patrol between the target and the other enemy airbase.

Example 1: A Heavily Defended Bridge

Suppose your orders specify a series of heavily defended bridges along the coastline in the northeast corner of the op zone. A large S-300 site and shorter-range systems defend the site. An enemy airfield is located 100 km to the southwest. You have available one A-50, four Su-27s, two MiG-27s and two Su-25s.

Obviously, the best ingress route is over water, where no stray SAMs wait to ambush the group. The MiG-27s can carry more Kh-31 anti-radiation missiles, so let them attack the SAM radars. Arm the Su-25s for a pinpoint strike with at least two Kh-29s per aircraft and order them to attack the bridges. Position the A-50 well outside the combat zone and over the water. The first pair of Su-27s should maintain a patrol between the enemy air base and the strike group's ingress route. The second group of Su-27s should fly fighter sweep over the main target just as the MiG-27s arrive.

Example 2: An Enemy Air Base

Your orders target the airbase at Sevastopol. It has an early warning radar, an S-300 system, and shorter-range Tunguska and Tor systems. Primary targets are the runways, hangars, and control towers. Grounded aircraft and fuel tanks are secondary objectives. You have available one A-50, six Su-27s, four S-24s, and two MiG-23s.

Obviously, you should position the A-50 over the water far to the south, out of harm's way. One pair of Su-27s should perform a combination fighter sweep and anti-radiation attack. The Su-27 can carry four Kh-31s along with two R-77s and two R-73s. As of version 1.0, anti-radiation missiles won't engage early warning radars. Therefore, the Su-27 pair should attack the S-300 search and track radar units, then use remaining Kh-31s against the Tunguska and Tor systems. The next pair of Su-27s should maintain a defensive position somewhat north and east of Sevastopol, intercepting any enemy fighters rallying from nearby bases. The last pair of Su-27s should perform wide escort for the Su-24s. One pair of Su-24s should be charged with destroying Sevastopol's runway while the other pair executes a pinpoint strike against the buildings and early warning radar. Station the MiG-23s as a reception escort or base CAP near the home airfield.

In conclusion, you'll never have enough aircraft available to cover all the bases, and there is always another bandit or SAM launcher waiting to ambush your forces. In all cases, you must make some sacrifices and leave some flanks unguarded. The trick, of course, is knowing which flank you can safely leave unattended. Mission intelligence reports offer some clues, but are never 100 percent accurate. As mission planner, you must make the hard decisions and live with your judgment calls.

APPENDIX A

Air-to-Air Weapons Comparison

Air-to-air missiles come in several varieties based on its guidance system. The earliest air-to-air missiles were *infrared* (IR) missiles. These homed in on the heat the target emitted. Early IR guidance systems weren't very sensitive, however, and could only track targets from directly behind. More modern IR missiles use more sensitive seekers capable of detecting heat emissions from any angle. These *all-aspect* IR missiles work significantly better than the older, *rear-aspect* missiles. IR missiles acquire the target from the launching platform prior to launch, then receive no further guidance information after leaving the rail. If the missile loses lock, it will target any new heat source it finds, regardless of political alliance. IR missiles are true fire-and-forget weapons, but great care must be taken to prevent inadvertently downing friendly aircraft.

Radar-guided missiles come in two varieties, *semi-active* and *active* guidance. Semi-active radar homing (SARH) missiles have no onboard radar transmitter. The launching aircraft must maintain a radar lock on the target until the missile strikes. The SARH missile tracks the radar's reflections off the target. Although SARH missiles have served for decades, reliance on the launching platform's radar lock offers severe disadvantages.

Active radar homing (ARH) missiles are a bit of a misnomer. Popular myth (and most flight simulations) portray them as fire-and-forget weapons using only onboard radar to seek out and destroy targets. All ARH missiles, including the vaunted AIM-54 Phoenix, actually use ARH guidance for only the terminal portion of the flight. The AIM-54 flies SARH for most of the flight, engaging its onboard radar when it closes to the target. The AIM-120 AMRAAM receives guidance information from the launching platform as long as it maintains a lock on the target. The AIM-120 steers to a point in space using inertial guidance, then activates its onboard radar for the final hunt-and-kill phase of the flight.

Missiles use a variety of warheads and fuses. While directly striking the target is the preferred option, it's difficult for a small missile to strike a maneuvering target dead center. Subsequently, modern missiles use expanding warheads and proximity fuses. If the missile senses it's as close as it's going to get to the target, it detonates the warhead anyway. Some warheads throw a large ball of shrapnel into the air, others extend a long, metal circle hoping to snag the target aircraft. More modern designs focus the explosion to direct the shrapnel toward the target.

Russian Missiles

For decades the West enjoyed a technological lead over the East in nearly every regard. By the mid-1980s, however, the playing field had leveled. Current missiles designed for the MiG-29 and Su-27 combat aircraft equal contemporary Western missiles in many respects and outperform them in other areas.

R-23 / AA-7 Apex

| R-23R | AA-7A Apex | SARH | 50km |
| R-23T | AA-7B Apex | IR | 25km |

The Apex is one of three later-generation Soviet air-to-air missiles that became known in the West in 1976. The Apex is roughly comparable to the American AIM-7 Sparrow. The Apex has clearly superior performance to its predecessor, the AA-3. Canard fins ahead of the wings and supplementary control surfaces near the rear of the missile provide exceptional maneuverability. Both missiles possess look-down, shoot-down capability against low-altitude targets.

Both radar-guided and IR versions make up the MiG-23's standard armament (as well as that of the MiG-21 and MiG-25). Range reports vary, generally specifying 30 to 50 km for the R-23R and 20 to 25 km for the R-23T. The R-23 carries a blast/fragmentation warhead with both proximity and impact fuses.

R-27 / AA-10 Alamo

R-27R	AA-10A Alamo A	SARH	80 km
R-27T	AA-10B Alamo B	IR	70 km
R-27RE	AA-10C Alamo C	SARH	130 km
R-27TE	AA-10D Alamo D	IR	120 km

The R-27 family was developed primarily for the MiG-29 and Su-27 warplanes. As with most Soviet-designed missiles, it comes in both radar-guided and heat-seeking variants. As usual, the radar-guided variant has longer range than the heat-seeking counterpart. The manual provides contradictory information regarding the range of the RE and TE variants, listing 100 km in some places. Other sources generally list the R and T variants with only an 8 km range and the RE and TE (usually called ER and ET) variants with a 30 km range. Since the R-27 was designed specifically to replace the older R-23, it seems unlikely it would have a shorter range than the older missile. The R-23 carries a blast/fragmentation warhead with both proximity and impact fuses.

R-33 / AA-9 Amos

R-33	AA-9 Amos	SARH	160 km

The primary weapon of the MiG-31 interceptor, this missile uses inertial guidance to the target and SARH guidance during terminal phase. *Su-27*'s version of this missile offers a 160 km range, although other sources indicate actual range is closer to 130 km. Although not available to *Su-27* players, the R-33 (listed in the manual as both R-33E and R-33A) has been seen on real-world Su-27s. This missile is arguably similar to the U.S. Navy's AIM-54 Phoenix;

both are intended to intercept large aircraft and cruise missiles at long range. Some reports indicate one R-33 variant carries a nuclear warhead.

R-60 / AA-8 Aphid

R-60	AA-8 Aphid	IR	10 km

The R-60 comes in R-60R (radar-guided) and R-60T (heat-seeking) variants, although *Su-27* contains only the R-60T version. A relatively small missile, the heat-seeking variant only reaches 10 km while the radar-guided variant extends to 15 km. Although one of the smallest missiles ever built, the R-60 is extremely agile and carries an effective fragmentation warhead with both proximity and impact fuses. Almost every Russian combat aircraft can carry the R-60, but it's quite inferior to the R-73 and the American AIM-9 Sidewinder.

R-73 / AA-11 Archer

R-73	AA-11 Archer	IR	40 km

The R-73 ushered in the era of Soviet missile superiority. Combining long range (for a heat-seeking missile) and off-boresight targeting capability, the R-73 gives Russian pilots more shot opportunities than the older R-60 or the American AIM-9. Coupled with its all-aspect attack capability, it's arguably one of the best heat-seeking missiles in the world, superior to the AIM-9 in many respects and comparable to the Israeli-built heat-seeking missiles. The R-73 uses an expanding-rod warhead.

R-77 / AA-12 Adder

R-77	AA-12 Adder	ARH	150 km

Dubbed the "AMRAAMski" by some Western analysts, this long-range, active-radar missile reportedly performs on a par with the U.S.'s AIM-120 AMRAAM. The R-77 is highly maneuverable, can attack from any aspect angle, resists ECM, and can track low-altitude targets against ground clutter. Coupled with the R-73, most Western analysts agree that modern Eastern missiles hold a significant advantage over current Western missiles.

American Missiles

For the most part, American missile design has stagnated. For years U.S. defense policy lived by the "not invented here" rule–that is, if it wasn't invented in the U.S. it wouldn't be used to defend the U.S. This policy, although stifling in some regards, ensured that military readiness never depended on relations with foreign countries.

The AIM-9 and AIM-7 soldiered on through frontline service for decades. Numerous upgrades improved performance, but clearly new missiles would be needed for the 21st century. While U.S. developers began work on the AIM-120 AMRAAM to replace the aging AIM-7, the U.S. strayed from its "not invented here" philosophy regarding heat-seeking missiles. The U.S. entered a partnership with several European nations to develop an advanced, short-range, heat-seeking missile. The European program slowed, then came to a halt, prompting the U.S. to withdraw. This, however, left the U.S. starting new AIM-9 development programs years after Russian forces deployed modern missiles. The AIM-120 AMRAAM evens the table for Western forces. To paraphrase, "This is not your father's missile."

AIM-9

AIM-9P	IR	17 km

Having served for nearly a half-century, the AIM-9 has proved itself on several battlefields. During the Vietnam War, the AIM-7 Sparrow suffered mediocre performance. Further, political constraints prevented aircrews from effectively operating the missile. With the F-4 lacking an internal cannon, the AIM-9 Sidewinder was forced to fill the gap. Years later, newer Sidewinders served with distinction during the Gulf War.

AIM-120

AIM-120	ARH	75 km

Generally speaking, when an AMRAAM is launched something will get hit. The AMRAAM stores target information prior to launch, then uses onboard intertial guidance to steer to a point in space. On arriving, it activates its onboard radar and searches for its target. The missile receives mid-course guidance instructions as long as the launching platform maintains lock. If the lock is broken for any reason, the missile continues under inertial guidance using the latest update from the launching aircraft.

APPENDIX B

Metric Conversion

Ultimately, to maximize Su-27 performance you must learn to fly using its metric measurements. Initially, however, those more accustomed to imperial units can perform rough approximations while learning the metric parameters.

Airspeed

Generally, divide kilometers-per-hour by 2 for a rough approximation of airspeed in knots. For example, 500 km/hr equates to approximately 267.6 kts. Dividing 500 km/hr by 2 results in 250 kts. Although not an exact figure, it provides a reasonably accurate estimation.

Altitude

Simply multiply altitude in meters by 3. While a meter is slightly more than 3 feet, this estimation provides a reasonably accurate estimation. For example, 10,000 meters equates to roughly 32,500 feet. Multiplying by 3 results in an estimated 30,000 feet. Again, not an accurate figure, but close enough for a tight situation.

Exact Conversions

To Convert From	To	Multiply By
Kilometers	Nautical Miles	.53
Km/Hr	Knots	.53
Nautical Miles	Kilometers	1.88
Knots	Km/Hr	1.88

Index

NOTES

NOTES

NOTES

Computer Game Books

1942: The Pacific Air War—The Official Strategy Guide	$19.95
The 11th Hour: The Official Strategy Guide	$19.95
The 7th Guest: The Official Strategy Guide	$19.95
Aces Over Europe: The Official Strategy Guide	$19.95
Across the Rhine: The Official Strategy Guide	$19.95
Alone in the Dark 3: The Official Strategy Guide	$19.95
Armored Fist: The Official Strategy Guide	$19.95
Ascendancy: The Official Strategy Guide	$19.95
Blackthorne: The Official Strategy Guide	$14.95
CD-ROM Games Secrets, Volume 1	$19.95
Celtic Tales: Balor of the Evil Eye—The Official Strategy Guide	$19.95
Cyberia: The Official Strategy Guide	$19.95
Computer Adventure Games Secrets	$19.95
Descent: The Official Strategy Guide	$19.95
DOOM Battlebook	$14.95
DOOM II: The Official Strategy Guide	$19.95
Dracula Unleashed: The Official Strategy Guide & Novel	$19.95
Dragon Lore: The Official Strategy Guide	$19.95
Dungeon Master II: The Legend of Skullkeep—The Official Strategy Guide	$19.95
Fleet Defender: The Official Strategy Guide	$19.95
Frankenstein: Through the Eyes of the Monster—The Official Strategy Guide	$19.95
Front Page Sports Football Pro '95: The Official Playbook	$19.95
Hell: A Cyberpunk Thriller—The Official Strategy Guide	$19.95
Heretic: The Official Strategy Guide	$19.95
I Have No Mouth, and I Must Scream: The Official Strategy Guide	$19.95
In The 1st Degree: The Official Strategy Guide	$19.95
The Journeyman Project 2: Buried in Time—The Official Strategy Guide	$19.95
Kingdom: The Far Reaches—The Official Strategy Guide	$14.95
King's Quest VII: The Unauthorized Strategy Guide	$19.95
The Legend of Kyrandia: The Official Strategy Guide	$19.95
Lords of Midnight: The Official Strategy Guide	$19.95
Machiavelli the Prince: Official Secrets & Solutions	$12.95
Marathon: The Official Strategy Guide	$19.95
Master of Orion: The Official Strategy Guide	$19.95
Master of Magic: The Official Strategy Guide	$19.95
Microsoft Arcade: The Official Strategy Guide	$12.95
Microsoft Flight Simulator 5.1: The Official Strategy Guide	$19.95

Video Game Books

3DO Game Guide	$16.95
Battle Arena Toshinden Game Secrets: The Unauthorized Edition	$12.95
Behind the Scenes at Sega: The Making of a Video Game	$14.95
Boogerman Official Game Secrets	$12.95
Breath of Fire Authorized Game Secrets	$14.95
Complete Final Fantasy III Forbidden Game Secrets	$14.95
Donkey Kong Country Game Secrets the Unauthorized Edition	$9.95
EA SPORTS Official Power Play Guide	$12.95
Earthworm Jim Official Game Secrets	$12.95
Killer Instinct Game Secrets: The Unauthorized Edition	$9.95
The Legend of Zelda: A Link to the Past—Game Secrets	$12.95
Lord of the Rings Official Game Secrets	$12.95
Maximum Carnage Official Game Secrets	$9.95
Mega Man X Official Game Secrets	$14.95
Mortal Kombat II Official Power Play Guide	$9.95
NBA JAM: The Official Power Play Guide	$12.95
GamePro Presents: Nintendo Games Secrets Greatest Tips	$11.95
Nintendo Games Secrets, Volumes 1, 2, 3, and 4	$11.95 each
Ogre Battle: The March of the Black Queen— The Official Power Play Guide	$14.95
Parent's Guide to Video Games	$12.95
Secret of Evermore: Authorized Power Play Guide	$12.95
Secret of Mana Official Game Secrets	$14.95
Sega CD Official Game Secrets	$12.95
GamePro Presents: Sega Genesis Games Secrets Greatest Tips, Second Edition	$12.95
Official Sega Genesis Power Tips Book, Volumes 2, and 3	$14.95 each
Sega Genesis Secrets, Volume 4	$12.95
Sega Genesis and Sega CD Secrets, Volume 5	$12.95
Sega Genesis Secrets, Volume 6	$12.95
Sonic 3 Official Play Guide	$12.95
Super Empire Strikes Back Official Game Secrets	$12.95
Super Mario World Game Secrets	$12.95
Super Metroid Unauthorized Game Secrets	$14.95
Super NES Games Secrets, Volumes 2, and 3	$11.95 each
Super NES Games Secrets, Volumes 4 and 5	$12.95 each
GamePro Presents: Super NES Games Secrets Greatest Tips	$11.95
Super NES Games Unauthorized Power Tips Guide, Volumes 1 and 2	$14.95 each
Super Star Wars Official Game Secrets	$12.95
Urban Strike Official Power Play Guide, with Desert Strike & Jungle Strike	$12.95

TO ORDER BOOKS

Please send me the following items:

Quantity	Title	Unit Price	Total
_____	_____	$_____	$_____
_____	_____	$_____	$_____
_____	_____	$_____	$_____
_____	_____	$_____	$_____
_____	_____	$_____	$_____
	_____	$_____	$_____

Subtotal	$_____
7.25% Sales Tax (CA only)	$_____
8.25% Sales Tax (TN only)	$_____
5.0% Sales Tax (MD only)	$_____
7.0% G.S.T. Canadian Orders	$_____
Shipping and Handling*	$_____
TOTAL ORDER	$_____

*$4.00 shipping and handling charge for the first book, and $1.00 for each additional book.

By telephone: With Visa or MC, call 1-916-632-4400. Mon.–Fri. 9–4 PST.

By mail: Just fill out the information below and send with your remittance to:

PRIMA PUBLISHING
P.O. Box 1260BK
Rocklin, CA 95677-1260

Satisfaction unconditionally guaranteed

Name_____

Address_____

City_____ State_____ Zip_____

Visa /MC#_____Exp._____

Signature_____